TT Contents

LEGENDS

FEATURES

Joey Dunlop

One of the many Dunlop TT celebrations. This is after winning the 1986 TTF1 race on the Rothmans Honda. (Don Morley)

Opposite Page: After a year out through serious injury, Joey returned to the Isle of Man in 1990. (Terry Howe)

Joey Dunlop has won more TT races than anyone in the 90-year history of the event, but racetrack fame has never altered the down-to-earth publican from Ballymoney.

Undisputed 'King of the Roads' he may be, but picking the darts out of the board at his bar on Ballymoney Station Joey Dunlop looks the unlikeliest of sporting heroes. The 45-year-old Ulsterman is known to enjoy a beer or two with his friends and customers, while shying away from the publicity that surrounds the greatest pure motorcycle road racer we've been privileged to witness.

In this modern sporting world of hype and self-praise many an average performer has been tagged king of their own particular sport. Most don't deserve such praise, but in the case of William Joseph Dunlop, the Ballymoney publican, such a title only tells half a story.

It was in 1976 that Dunlop started his own personal battle with the 37.73-mile Mountain Circuit on the Isle of Man. Twenty one years and 21 TT victories later this year he is contemplating perhaps his last racing visit to a circuit that he could almost claim as his own personal property. Typically, that last TT from the saddle will not be a sedate affair but a five-race programme

"The big factor is enjoyment and I have enjoyed my racing at the TT over the last few years like I never have before."

Unassuming HERO

including a ride on a 500cc NSR500 V-twin grand prix racing machine in the Senior race, which could be his very last appearance on the Mountain Circuit.

Dunlop started that amazing record-breaking victory run in 1977. I remember sitting at Ballaugh Bridge watching him in action that afternoon on the 750cc Yamaha winning the Jubilee Classic TT. Little did I, or probably many others, think that we would be returning to the Isle of Man 20 years later to watch Dunlop chasing his 22nd, or even 23rd or 24th TT victory. Great riders, we are told, can win races on any machinery, and just a glance at Dunlop's victory scroll would bear out that particular theory.

Following that initial victory on the 750 Yamaha two-stroke, Dunlop has ▶

Joey Dunlop *Unassuming Hero*

Joey Dunlop at Ramsey on the TZ750 Rea Racing Yamaha during his record-breaking run in the 1977 Jubilee Classic TT.

Opposite page: And just to show any doubters the 'old boy' can still cut it on the big bikes, Joey won the Senior TT on an RC45 Honda in 1995. during the same race week he also took the Lightweight honours with an RS250. (Terry Howe)

displayed his brilliance on a range of machinery, ranging from the four-stroke monsters to 125 two-stroke twins. Last year Dunlop won both the 125 and 250cc races on the Isle of Man, but picking his favourite victory is not easy.

"My victory in the 1980 Classic race was my most memorable because I beat all the factory riders by fooling them after fitting a 32-litre tank, which meant I could do three laps before stopping for fuel," revealed Dunlop.

"Another good memory is the first time I won the 125cc race in 1992, which equalled Mike Hailwood's record of 14 TT victories. I'd never been classed as a 125 rider, but it was good to go out there and beat my brother Robert after he had won that race for the previous three years. I even broke the lap record to prove it was no fluke."

That 1980 Classic victory came three years after his first triumph. Dunlop then had to wait another three years and in 1983 secured his third TT win and his first in the TT Formula One race. It started an incredible run of six

consecutive Formula One victories which was only broken when he was forced to miss the 1989 race because of injury, ironically sustained at Brands Hatch and not on a road circuit.

Dunlop started racing in 1970 on a Triumph Tiger Cub, in between working as lorry driver, a steel erector, a roofer and later as a very popular publican. He bought the 199cc four-stroke for £50 and was soon making his mark on the Irish roads that have provided such a proving ground for many an aspiring TT or Manx Grand Prix rider. His first trip to the Isle of Man resulted in three replicas in the three races he contested, but it was only a year later that familiar trips down victory lane to the winner's enclosure began. It is usually accompanied by a few modest words and, until a couple of years ago, a lighted cigarette.

In so many ways Dunlop typifies what the TT is all about. He is the king of the decreasing band of riders who are still prepared to take on the ultimate challenge of the TT Mountain Circuit.

It takes a very special person to race against the clock on a circuit that is renowned for being dangerous and which has a well-publicised record of serious accidents.

"The big factor is enjoyment and I have enjoyed my racing at the TT over the last few years like I never have before," explained the record breaker. "It's always a challenge to me in two ways, both riding and preparing my own bikes. I always look forward to the TT and if I did not enjoy it, I would not go back. I think I must know every inch of the circuit by now. To win races there you have to be consistent. Some people can put in fast laps but not win races."

It's not only winning races that has made Joey Dunlop such a national hero back home in Northern Ireland and the first British motorcycle racer to be graced with both the MBE and the OBE in the Queen's New Year's Honours list. He was made an MBE for his racing exploits. The award of the OBE came in recognition of his solo mercy mis-

sions to Bosnia, Albania and Romania. Typically, this shy family man does not talk much about his missions to help youngsters less fortunate than his own five children Julie, Donna, Garry, Richard and Joanne, although he does admit his TT-winning exploits have helped him out of difficult situations, a long way from home.

"On the way back from Albania I was arrested at gunpoint for not having the correct documents," recalled Dunlop. "They wanted £25 from me to cross the checkpoint but I would not pay. I gave them some racing stickers and motor-cycling papers. The Chief of Police happened to be a motor sport fan, so he wrote me a letter allowing me to continue." With the backing of his wife Linda he has continued his trips that started after he watched the sad plight of orphaned children in Bosnia. "I saw the troubles on television and decided to help out. The food and clothes were donated locally and I drove around the area of my home collecting them and then set off when the van was full."

The TT races without Joey Dunlop heading the entry list could seem a very strange place in 1998 although 'yer maun', as he is known throughout Northern Ireland, may still consider retirement a decision for the future rather than the present. Arguments, usually over a pint of Manx ale, will continue on who is the greatest TT rider of all time. The late, great Mike Hailwood won 14 TT races, combining magnificent performances on both road circuits such as the Isle of Man and Grand Prix tracks throughout the world. Dunlop has never pretended that he enjoyed short circuit racing, but I'm sure even Hailwood would admit that Dunlop has rightly earned the crown as the undisputed 'King of the Roads'.

Words: *Nick Harris*

> *"My victory in the 1980 Classic race was my most memorable because I beat all the factory riders by fooling them after fitting a 32-litre tank."*

Norton 588cc

Right: Hislop's ABUS Norton TT winner — 588cc, water-cooled twin-rotor rotary engine producing 147bhp at 10,000rpm. (Alan Cathcart Archive)

Steve Hislop's 1992 Senior TT winner

It was the closest, most exciting Senior TT for years and Steve Hislop was on a Norton rotary when he pipped Carl Fogarty by seconds. As far as the TT was concerned, it was the British marque's last stand.

When super-Scot Steve Hislop crossed the line to clinch victory in the 1992 Senior TT from Yamaha-mounted Carl Fogarty, it was the first TT success for the British manufacturer since 1973, when Peter Williams won the F750 race on the monocoque JPN.

The 1992 Senior was run at an electrifying pace, with the lead see-sawing between Foggy and 'Hizzie', neither of them more than eight seconds ahead on corrected time for the entire six-lap race. The Norton rider lost time during his second pit stop with a filler-cap that wouldn't close, leaving him three seconds adrift of the Yamaha at Glen Helen on the penultimate lap. But a superhuman effort saw him retake the lead by

six seconds as he started the last lap.

Both riders broke the record on the run to the flag, 'Foggy' setting a new record at 123.61mph. But it wasn't enough, and Hislop took the honours with 4.4s to spare. Hislop's one-off TT ride was on a works Norton leased by bike security specialists ABUS from the team's regular sponsors, John Player Special, who had foolishly not budgeted for the Island event. Hislop was forced to make many set-up changes compared to Ron Haslam's short-circuit machine to make the twin-rotary work around the 37.73 mile course — softer suspension settings, higher ride height and a more conservative steering head angle. Yet he still struggled with a bike that was overheating and handling badly in his first

…ht: Inverted 41mm front forks were by WP and …kes were twin 310mm PVM ventilated cast-iron …ors gripped by four-piston AP callipers. Michelin …es were used front and rear on PVM rims. Rear …ck was by Koni/Maxton. (Alan Cathcart Archive)

Below Right: A rotary engine sat in a twin-spar aluminium alloy frame fabricated to Norton spec by Harris Performance. By 1992, Norton had adopted the six-speed FZR1000 gear cluster. Primary drive was by toothed belt. Power went through a dry, 18-plate clutch with diaphragm spring. Where was the Hislop replica streetbike? (Alan Cathcart Archive)

Farewell to Arms

race, the TTF1, on Saturday. However, by Friday, after several more chassis changes and after adopting a more relaxed riding style, he was right on the pace to score a memorable victory. Sadly, Norton never followed up the achievement. The TT winner went off to the National Motorcycle Museum and the TT organisers did not encourage Colin Seeley's Duckhams Norton outfit to the Island. Another chapter closed on British motorcycle racing history.

Far Right: Steve Hislop flicks 144kg of rompin', stompin' British thoroughbred through Keppel on his way to a glorious victory in the 1992 Senior TT. (Terry Howe)

Mick Boddice

Boddice and Wells at Parliament Square, Ramsey, during the 1992 TT on the Castrol Honda. (Terry Howe)

It was a long time coming, but once Mick Boddice achieved his first Sidecar TT victory in 1983, with Chas Birks in the chair, the floodgates opened and he's now got nine TT wins to his credit, equalling the record of German ace, Siegfreid Schauzu and Dave Saville.

Until last year, when arch rival, Dave Molyneux went on a record-breaking spree, Boddice held the fastest ever TT Sidecar lap at 108.31mph, set in 1989 on a 700 Yamaha, and the fastest race average at 107.17mph set in the Sidecar B race, also in 1989.

Boddice has also taken three British Championship titles on short circuits — all coming in recent years. Now 49-years-old, Boddice reckons he's improv-ing with age: "I'm just like vintage wine," he quips.

This year, chasing a record-breaking tenth win, will be his 31st TT. It was always decreed that Boddice would fall in love with the Mountain course. He travelled across the Irish Sea many times as a youngster when his father, Bill raced at the TT. "My first visit was in 1954 and we stayed at the Nursery Hotel on the side of the old Clypse Course with people like Eric Oliver, Cyril Smith and Jacques Drion who had a female passenger, Inga Stoll," says Mick. "There was always this lure of the TT. I suppose it was because I'd been going with him [his father] for so long it was bound to overtake my life."

Nine years later young Boddice start-ed his own track career: "It was Good Friday at Brands Hatch,1963. I rode one of the old man's Manx Nortons on the long circuit. I finished third in a handicap race and won £15. I went and bought a pair of Agostini-style gog-gles!"

On the short circuits, Mick, in his early racing career, was one among a quartet of BSA outfits dominating the British short-circuit scene. An appren-tice at BSA he recalls four great years in the competition department.

"Going to work at BSA was like going to a club rather than work," he states. "Most of the people in the comp shop, like Peter Brown, Chris Vincent, Norman Hanks, and myself all used to race. It was quite competitive. You'd

Exploiting the DRIVE

With F2 Sidecars it's all about getting the power down — and no one is more experienced at it than Mick Boddice, veteran of nine TT victories.

quite important — especially after Vincent had won a TT on a BSA [back in 1962]."

Mick recalls that his Sidecar TT debut got off to something of a false start: "It was 1966. I'd built myself up for June but there was a seaman's strike so I had to wait until August. We had a special fuel tank made up, slung under the floorpan. But we picked a stray bolt. It punched a hexagon hole and all the fuel ran out. It wasn't much of a debut at all!

"The following year, though, we managed to finish joint eighth — with Arsenius Butscher and he had our engine measured as well. He couldn't believe a 500 BSA could do it."

While solo racing was forging ahead with new technology, thanks to the Japanese factories and their exotic works bikes, sidecar outfits back then were best described as basic, as Boddice explains: "We had Manx Norton frames cut down and lowered and Ken Sprayson used to make a pair of leading link forks for it and away we went."

At that time, schoolmate, Dave Loach was Boddice's racing accomplice. The partnership ended when Loach crashed a road bike and broke both wrists. Clive Pollington took over on the platform.

be working on a cylinder head at 10pm so no one could see what you were doing."

Mick followed his father's footsteps to the European GPs. In addition to the TT, Bill used to take in the Dutch and Belgium events and that's how Mick started. "In those days we used to turn up and do a GP. In 1967 we took the BSA to the Dutch and I finished eighth quite early on in my career."

The organisers, under pressure from the German crews, had it measured. "All the Germans came around to check this poor little BSA, he says. "Then we went on to Spa on the old fast circuit. I arranged for Pip Harris to tow me around and did 102mph in practise." The speeds were unheard of for a 500cc

A50 with a four-speed box! They measured it again.

"The GPs were a real good experience. Later on I did five full seasons of Grands Prix with the Yamaha and finished on the rostrum several times."

Keen as Mick might have been about those continental trips, it was the TT that was always top of the agenda. Why was racing around the 37.73-mile road course so crucial? He recalls: "When I started it was so important for sponsorship — what little there was. If you won a silver replica at the TT you used to get bonuses. Shell, Dunlop, plug people, Renold chain, all gave money or products, or worked something out for you. And then it was a Grand Prix anyway. With BSA it was

ACTION! The Best Video

Agostini - Profile of a Legend

PROFILE OF A LEGEND
DUKE

In 1965 a shrewd count Agusta signed up Giacomo Agostini. Having showed a serious interest in motorcycling racing at an early age, Agostini became fifteen times World Champion. This enthralling video captures the magic of Agostini.
60 mins. £12.99

Castrol History of Motorcycling 1

Volume 1
How It All Began & The TT

See early road races in Britain and on the continent with action from Brooklands, racing in France and also the first TT races in the Isle Of Man. Solid tyres, beltdrives and pedal assistance provide a fascinating video on how it all began.
60 mins. £10.99

Castrol History of Motorcycling 2

Volume 2
Birth of the GP & The Japanese Arrival

This video traces the 40-year history of world championship motorcycle racing. The works teams of Norton, Gilera, Guzzi, MV Agusta, BMW, AJS including footage of early Japanese appearances in Europe.
72 mins. £10.99

Castrol History of Motorcycling 3

Volume 3
The Other Champions
& Pressure, Money & The Need To Win

Other than the Blue Riband 500cc championship, the lightweights from 50cc to 350cc, and the sidecar racers had many worthy champions over the years - several of whom are featured in this episode.
£10.99

Classic Racer Experience

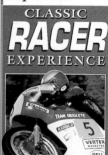

CLASSIC RACER EXPERIENCE
THRILLING RIDING & GREAT SOUNDS!
DUKE

The 37 mile TT Mountain brings thrills and chills to the heart of every rider. Now you can share the thrill of the TT course as experienced by the riders of single cylinder racers of the 1950's and '60's.
30 mins. £12.99

TT Classic Magic '96

DUKE

Where better to celebrate the glory days of AERMACHHI, NSU, VELOCETTE, SCOTT, AJS, MANX NORTON & Moto Guzzi than on the Isle Of Man TT. A marvellous tribute to the golden days of motorcycling on Magic Mountain.
85 mins. £10.99

Multi-Cylinder Magic

DUKE

In the summer of 1995, America's Team Obsolete revisited the legendary circuits of Mallory Park, Assen and Scarborough to relive the magic sights and sounds of multi-cylinder racing.
75 mins. £12.99

Champions Mike Hailwood

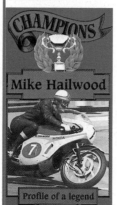

CHAMPIONS
Mike Hailwood
Profile of a legend

Undoubtedly one of the all-time great motorcycle racers, Mike Hailwood. We trace Mike's outstanding career from winning three TT's in 1961 when he was only 21 years old, through 9 World Championship.
58 mins. £12.99

Daytona'96 - Return of the Legend

DAYTONA CLASSICS '96
Return of the LEGENDS
DUKE

In 1996 over half a million bike fans flocked to Florida. Classic bike fans have their own good reasons to visit the Sunshine State and this year it was to witness the 'return of the legends'.
60 mins. £12.99

How to Order

Mick Boddice Exploiting the Drive

1907
1917
1927
1937
1947
1957
1967
1977
1987
1997

It was not until 1978 that Boddice finally stepped up onto the TT podium but he came close in 1969 with Pollington on the BSA. "After finishing the race, we came back up the pit road and were waved off into the winner's enclosure because they thought we had finished third. Then the timekeepers rang down to say Bill Currie had finished third on the Weslake.

"In those days there were no signals out around the course and no Manx Radio. You were just riding around blind. When I was working for BSA we used to take a handful of coins to Parliament Square during the solo races, do some hand timing and then frantically phone through to tell the Grandstand what the position was. Everyone used to do it. There were long queues at the phone box."

Not afraid of innovation, Boddice opted to race a three-cylinder BSA in 1970 after several years relying on an A65 twin. An oil leak sidelined them. He also tried another triple, a two-stroke Kawasaki 500 motor which he borrowed from brother-in-law Dave Simmonds, but development stopped when Dave was sadly killed at Rungis when Jack Findlay's caravan blew up.

If the Kawasaki was 'finicky,' it was nothing compared to the infamous Konigs, Boddice raced in 1974 and 1975. "Now they were unreliable," says Mick. "But they were also so quick to what we had been using. You'd have a problem but be keen to fix it because it was so fast. If you left the motor standing more than three minutes after a race all the water would run into the crankcases because the cases were porous. If we did manage to keep it running, we were forced to use gearboxes designed for Manx Nortons and 50bhp but were probably pushing 80-90 through the gearbox.

Above: Signpost, 1969 TT. Clive Pollington gives it the elbow on the BSA. (Nick Nicholls/Boddice collection)

Below: Wot, only two wheels? Boddice at age eight and a half, riding an Excelsior. (Boddice collection)

We kept breaking gearboxes.

"One year I did 20 races and finished with a third at the Belgian GP and a win at the Stars of Darley. We could have won at Spa but the temperature gauge packed up and I thought it was overheating. I called at the pits for water and rejoined in eighth but missed second place by inches on the line.

"It got to me in the end. I was going to pack up, but two brothers in Kidderminster, where I live, had a 700 Yamaha which I knew was pretty competitive. In desperation I asked if I could have a ride on it. I rode it up the Silverstone runway at 8,000rpm and thought, 'Christ, no wonder Dick Greasley [who had just switched to a Yamaha] could clear off so easily!'

"We did three end-of-season meetings and it was so good. The following year Roy Woodhouse's brother quit, so Roy sponsored me with Charlie Birks in the chair. We won the first ever [return] meeting at Donington and went two seasons unbeaten there."

Mick's first TT with the Yamaha was in 1977 — and four-lap races. "We knew we had to do a pit stop and

1907

1917

1927

1937

1947

1957

1967

1977

1987

1997

Mick Boddice Exploiting the Drive

Dave Loach puts some meaning into the expression, 'Body English' as he helps Mick Boddice get the BSA A50's power down out of the Gooseneck in 1967. (Nick Nicholls)

decided to keep the revs to 10,000, hoping that everyone would break down — but they never did. We managed two fifth places which we were quite pleased with, and the following year we got our first rostrum, second to Steinhausen."

The Boddice and Birks partnership has clocked up the most joint wins at the TT, six together. The first win came in 1983. Boddice says: "It was uneventful, until we started down the Glencrutchery Road to take the flag and then I started crying and couldn't stop. It was pure pleasure crying. I'd finally done what I wanted to do."

The Boddice/Birks combination ended in 1989 after the pair had won their third race in two years. Birks had been back to his best in 1988 after missing the previous year through injury.

Boddice explains why he teamed up with Donny Williams in 1987 to claim yet another win: "Chas fell out at Greeba in 1986. I turned right and he fell out. He had the flu that day and wasn't right at all. I arrived at Greeba Castle, turned into the left and it was touch and go whether I crashed or not. The hardest part was running back. I didn't know what to expect. I knew where he had crashed and luckily it was only a broken leg. It could have been far worse!"

It was a bad break though and Birks had a lot of metal work inserted. "When Chas raced again it was to prove to himself that he could still do it," says Boddice. Birks' departure coincided with the introduction of Formula Two Sidecars as the TT feature class, and a new partner for Boddice in Dave Wells.

Boddice recalls his disappointment at the demise of the 750s: "I was sick that they got rid of the big outfits. I envis-

aged small bikes, no power. We had been used to these monsters — 750cc, 16 gallons of fuel — and all of a sudden we're there with under-powered little bikes.

"In fact it was just the opposite. There were corners at the TT where you were taking more risks by not shutting off to keep the speed up down the straights! And in tighter corners like Governor's, Ramsey Hairpin, Gooseneck, you were actually coming out quicker because you weren't spinning the rear wheel. First time at Governor's it caught me out, lifted the front wheel and shot across the pavement. There was so much drive.

"I teamed up with Dave and used a Honda for the first year of F2. Dave had passengered for Neil Smith. We've been together ever since.

"The arrival of F2 was when we started playing around with suspension settings — instead of sliding everywhere you were driving. The class is a lot more technical now. It's so much cheaper too. We put the Honda in and it did the season. It had 33,000 miles on it before the TT — it was an old press bike engine! All we did was have the head off, port it and borrow a set of carbs and off we went to the TT and finished second.

"Honda were fairly impressed. Honda Japan got to hear about it — the TT is still important to them — and I ended up with a brand new engine, spares budget, all sorts of things."

Boddice has been supported directly by Honda since — and continues to race an Ireson chassis which suits his hard-charging style that calls for plenty of grip from the front end.

As well as his own racing, Boddice has been able to chart the progress of his son's career. It all began with Mick

Jnr sharing a bike with his dad. It meant that up to 1995, the youngster had only done three full seasons of racing — yet he still finished fourth in the British championship. And thus far, with only two TTs under his belt, Junior has impressed everyone. In 1995 he won best newcomers and then he finished 11th last year — averaging 102mph. A chip off the old block?

Mick Jnr's best lap would have been race-winning pace in 1992, which underlines the rapid progress being made in the class.

Boddice Snr points out: "We didn't even have a race kit the first time we went F2. As far as development goes, it's been a bit of trial and error — a bit like the BSA days, some things work, some don't, but you are taking a road engine and modifying it. The difference now [since F2] is that we can go a full season on an engine — including the TT — with just oil changes!"

"The other tricky thing was changing from the big outfits to the 600. You used to brake early and accelerate though the corner. With the Honda, you brake later and accelerate earlier to keep the corner speed up. It's a lot more fun now, especially since Honda got involved. It's lifted the profile of sidecar racing.

"We're not getting hardly any more horsepower now than the we did in the second year of the Honda. We got to 100bhp and that's it — chassis development and tyre development are where the gains are now. Racing is closer these days so we all have to do this. We're exploiting the drive now rather than the wheelspin."

With so many TT experiences to call upon, Boddice doesn't plump for his first win but goes for his first ton-up lap as the outstanding memory: "We didn't finish the race, we broke down at Ballaugh, but I felt like I'd reached a landmark.

A puncture stopped us. I remember asking just about everyone if we had done the 100mph lap. Then a marshal came over and said it had just been announced. I was so pleased.

Even after all these years, he still looks forward to the TT and says: "I'll keep going until I stop enjoying it. It's not possible to carry on at this level unless you are enjoying it.

"And I enjoy short circuit probably more now than ever before. There, and at the TT, young lads are trying to beat me. Fisher beat me last year and said, 'at last, I've beaten the old man of racing'. He was chuffed to beat me but I was chuffed to know his goal was to beat me."

Words: *Gary Pinchin*

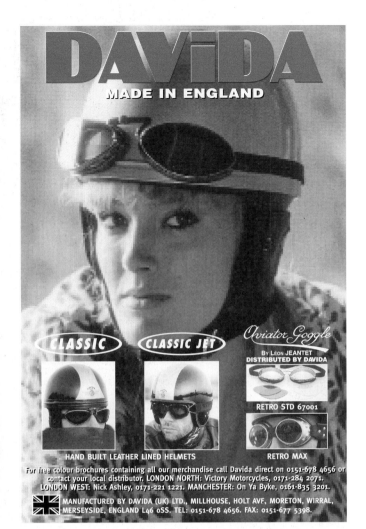

Sounds of the Sixties

Bill Ivy at Whitegates on the four-cylinder 250cc Yamaha in 1967. (Nick Nicholls)

Screaming multis, screeching two-strokes, throbbing singles. The 1960s was an era of intense motorcycle development — and the TT was the ideal testing ground for all this new technology.

It was not just names such as Agostini, Anderson, Hailwood, Hartle, Hocking, Ivy, McIntyre, Minter, Read, Surtees and Taveri gracing the TT results that made the 1960s one of the most memorable decades in the Isle of Man's racing history. It was also the sounds of vastly contrasting machines like the howling MVs, the screaming Honda multis, the screeching Yamahas and the throbbing Norton and G50 Matchless singles that helped to bring it to the fore.

However, the period will be remembered for the full-scale arrival of the Japanese factories that went from also-rans to winners in just three years before completely dominating the grand prix spectrum within six. ▶

Ernst Degner flat-out at Bray Hill to fourth place in the 1966 on this 50cc Suzuki. (Nick Nicholls)

Six-cylinders and third place for Ralph Bryans on the 250cc during the 1967 TT. (Nick Nicholls)

Honda

SOUNDS OF THE SIXTIES

Ralph Bryans aviates the tiny 50cc Honda over Ballaugh ahead of Suzuki's Morishita in 1964. They finished second and third respectively. (Nick Nicholls)

Honda SOUNDS OF THE SIXTIES

Japanese mechanics work on a pair of Honda fours. The pic is taken at the Belgian GP in 1966. (Mick Woollett Archive)

When Honda arrived on the Island for its TT debut in 1959 it raised more than a few smiles as it unloaded its production 125cc machines at its Onchan headquarters — they were fitted with 'knobbly' tyres!

However, with more suitable rubber for the last Lightweight TT, run on the Clypse Course, the machines quickly gained respect. While the twin-cylinder four-strokes were no speed match for the established MVs, Ducatis and MZs in the class, their reliability was rewarded with the manufacturer's team prize.

None of Honda's five riders had any Isle of Man experience but three of them, headed by Namoi Tanaguchi, filled sixth, seventh and eighth places at the end of the ten-lap 107.9 mile race.

Encouragement indeed for the Honda factory which first took a look at TT racing five years previously when enthusiastic boss Soichiro Honda joined the spectators and then continued to research the sport for a number of years via an 'army' of camera-equipped technicians.

Even after a year of intensive development the re-vamped 125 Honda for the 1960 TT did not provide any threat to the supremacy of the MV and MZ works machines. Once more they proved reliable, filling sixth to tenth positions with Tanaguchi again heading the pack and with Australian Tom Phillis, one of the first non-Japanese riders to be enlisted, bringing up the rear. It was pretty obvious that full account had not been given to the major differences between the Clypse and the more demanding and varied 37.75 Mountain Course.

Honda also entered the 250 arena with impressive-looking four-cylinder machinery which unfortunately did not take to the tough course. The 'fours' featured a complex 16-valve system,

with downdraught carburettors and produced around 35bhp at 14,500rpm.

Aussie Bob Brown, who rode a Honda for the first time in practise after taking over the four allocated to Tanaka, managed to head Moto Kitano and Tanaguchi over the line in fourth place but he was almost six minutes behind Tarquinio Provini's winning Morini.

Then came the start of the take-over. The following year, after much time at the drawing board and in the development department, Honda arrived with a new set of machines and captured the first five places in both the 125 and 250 races.

The smaller class gave Mike Hailwood his first TT victory by just two seconds from Luigi Taveri, who was followed home by Phillis, Jim Redman and Sadao Shimazaki. Hailwood added win number two in the 250 race ahead of Phillis, Redman, Tagahashi and Taniguchi.

Bob McIntyre, lapped at 99.50 mph — faster than John Surtees' 350 MV record — on lap two, but then slowed before going out with an oil leak on the final lap at Quarry Bends. With Gary Hocking's MV already parked, Hailwood was home and almost dry in damp conditions.

Honda was demonstrating a sound development policy at this stage. In 1960 it produced a completely new machine without deviating from it basic original principles and in 1961 set about the handling problem by discarding a 'spine' frame in favour of one more along the lines of the Norton Featherbed — although the engine still formed an integral part of the structure and the top of the steering head column was braced to the tank by a single tube. The engine with gear-driven, dohc and a bore and stroke of 44mm x 41mm — a double-up of the 125 twin — was giving 44bhp at 14,000rpm.

Alterations to the valve size and timing brought the lower limit of the 250 fours in 1962 down to 10,000rpm, with 46bhp on tap. The diameter of the twin leading shoe front brakes was increased by 20mm and, because the race distance had be extended to six laps, 7.9 gallon fuel tanks were fitted for a non-stop run. However, because of the top weight when full, the idea of using them was abandoned after practise.

Derek Minter won the race after battling with Redman who made a precautionary pit stop at the end of lap five because fuel was spewing out of a loose tank cap.

However, the Honda technicians were worried by misfiring problems that put McIntyre — using new Dunlop 'triangular' tyres — out after leading on the

The 125-5 Honda, 22,000rpm, eight-speed gearbox and 34bhp — ace-mechanic, Nobby Clarke, who worked on these bikes, reckons it's the noisiest bike ever. (Mick Woollett Archive)

first lap, ended Kitano's at School House and slowed third placed Phillis.

The team spent a day sorting out the trouble at Jurby and were late weighing-in their 125 and Junior race machines.

They had entirely new production Benly racers for Minter, Phillis and Sadao Shimazaki which were developed from the twin-cylinder race engine. Features included magneto ignition, twin Keihin carbs and five-speed gearbox. With the overhead camshafts driven by spur gears from the left end of the crankshaft, the engines produced 20bhp at 13,500rpm. Taveri and Tommy Robb, on pukka racers, took first and second places ahead of Phillis, Minter, and Redman who was down to one cylinder.

For their entry in the 350 race Honda used enlarged 250 machines — that came up to 285cc — for McIntyre, who went out at Kepple Gate on the second lap with engine failure. Phillis died on the same lap when he crashed at Laurel Bank while running third.

For the first-ever 50cc TT Honda had to give best to Suzuki despite producing an eight-speed gearbox to replace the initial six-speeder in less than three weeks. The maximum rpm was increased to 14,000 for the single after experimenting with different bore and stroke configurations.

Redman claimed his first TT win in the 1963 250 race, but with his four-stroke four he had a tougher than expected time against the much improved two-stroke Yamahas.

Redman scored his second win in the Junior on a full-size 350-4 which had a six-speed box and a 49mm x 45mm engine that produced 54bhp at 12,500rpm. The Hondas were outpaced by the Suzukis in the 125 race with Taveri best in fourth, while in the 50cc race there was no works support.

Only eight of 65 starters survived the 250 race in 1964 which was won by Redman on a four, but Taveri was sidelined by electrical troubles on a similar machine. It was Redman again — easily — in the Junior, when the luckless Taveri failed to start after his mechanics gave up the battle to cure a serious oil leak.

Honda was back in command of the 125 department for which it wheeled out new four-cylinder machines that revved to 16,000rpm, had eight-speed boxes and were speed-checked at almost 130mph. Taveri did the winning, to the surprise of second-placed Redman, and Ulsterman Ralph Bryans was third. Again more cylinders were brought into play in the 50cc race but the twin — that revved to around

20,000rpm, had a ten-speed box to deal with a narrow power-band and could hit the 100mph mark — was still not good enough to beat the Suzuki of Hugh Anderson. And that was despite a searing last lap effort from Bryans who went from sixth to snatch second place by 0.6s from Suzuki's Isao Morishita.

Honda's machinery got even more exotic the following year when Redman again clinched a 250/350 double. The 250 had a six-cylinder engine with a 39mm x 45.5mm bore and stroke that developed 53bhp and had a seven-speed box. But he wouldn't have had such an easy win if Phil Read's Yamaha had lasted for more than a lap.

With an updated 350-4, Redman repeated his winning performance in the Junior but only after tailing Mike Hailwood for the three laps who then went out with chain problems on his MV. Bruce Beale who injured his arm in a 125 race crash was fourth on his four. Honda lost out in the 125cc race when Yamaha's Read pipped Taveri but then the Swiss rider broke Suzuki's 50cc domination and gave Honda a first win in the class. Hailwood returned to Honda in 1966 when the factory went in search of Senior race honours for the first time — and promptly delivered the goods. The 500 Honda-4 produced an impressive 90bhp at 12,700rpm and the 57 mm x 48mm engine followed Honda's normal four-cylinder practice of mounting the engine across the frame.

Hailwood always complained about the poor handling of the multi's, despite various chassis set-ups and designs, although this has been questioned by Redman in recent years after he rode a 500 of the original design in Japan last year. Hailwood was sidelined in the Junior on the first lap at Bishopscourt by a faulty magneto, so Honda missed out to MV in that one, but it was Honda

1-2 domination in the 250cc race through Hailwood and Stuart Graham on six-cylinder machines.

Three, five-cylinder machines spearheaded Honda's effort in the 125 race but two of them were to fall victims of a rapid change in weather conditions. Taveri was competitive until he lost half a minute with a slip-road excursion at Ballacraine where conditions were damp. The bikes of Hailwood and Ralph Bryans were way down on power. The reason it seems was an over-rich mixture because the mechanics had anticipated a cool, damp morning race but, after a three-hour delay because of fog, a warm, dry air stream made its way across the Island.

Hailwood, Bryans and Taveri were sixth, seventh and eighth. Honda claimed nine of the top 12 places in the 50cc race — a massed start on that occasion — with Bryans just getting the better of Taveri to claim his first TT win. Honda pulled out of the 50 and 125cc classes in 1967, and the Diamond Jubilee TT was the swan-song of its official support in the 1960s. Hailwood took Honda out in a blaze of glory. He claimed the Senior honours on the four from a luckless MV-mounted Ago.

Earlier in the week he had blasted to the Lightweight race, setting new race and lap records and he dominated the Junior with a 297cc Honda that was virtually a bored-out 250cc six with a 44mm x 37.5mm bore and stroke.

Honda pulled out of grand prix racing at the end of the season — and that meant no more Honda exotica at the TT in the late 1960s. ▶

Hailwood and the six-cylinder Hondas dominated the 1967 TT in the Lightweight and Junior races. The '350' was virtually a bored-out 250 with a 44mm x 37.5mm bore and stroke. (Mick Woollett Archive)

Suzuki
SOUNDS OF THE SIXTIES

Stuart Graham on the 125
Suzuki during 1967 at
Ramsey. (Nick Nicholls)

Suzuki arrived on the Island a year after Honda to contest the Ultra Lightweight three-lapper with a racing version of the 125cc Colleda two-stroke twin. The engine had a conventional piston port design with a 44mm x 41mm bore and stroke, a six-bearing crankshaft assembly, a six-speed gearbox and could reach around 16,000rpm

Three Japanese national riders were due to race the RT60s but when Mitsuo Itoh was injured after crashing at the Bungalow during practise his place was taken by experienced British rider Ray Fay. Toshio Matsumoto claimed a bronze replica with 15th place, while Michio Inchino and Fay were 16th and 18th. The TT was the only event Suzuki contested in Europe that year, because it set about preparing a return to the Island the following year with 125 and 250cc machines.

Although the 125 retained a flywheel magneto ignition system and still ran on a petrol-oil mix, it now had a rotary disc-valve and a rather delicate positive-stop gearchange mechanism.

A series of machine problems during practise resulted in Suzuki withdrawing its three star players, South African Paddy Driver, New Zealander Hugh Anderson and Scot Alastair King, who had been signed just for the TT, from the 125 race in which they did not have a single finisher.

The scaled-up 56mm x 50.5mm version of the twin that was run in the 250cc race fared better with Anderson taking a bronze in tenth place and Inchino 12th. The other two bikes dnf'ed.

Suzuki decided that if it was to produce competitive racing machines it needed expertise from outside its own R&D department. This was to come from Ernst Degner who was racing for MZ, the acknowledged leader of two-stroke development — luckily, he was anxious to defect from East Germany.

The expertise and technical information he took to Suzuki quickly paid dividends and the factory gained its first TT win in the newly-introduced 50cc class of 1962.

Fittingly, it was Degner who took the honours with a single-cylinder disc-valve two-stroke machine that developed almost 10bhp between 11 and 12,000rpm and had an eight-speed gearbox. And while he buzzed his way to an 18s victory over Taveri's Honda, Mitsuo Itoh and Michio Ichino made fifth and sixth places to secure the manufacturer's team award for Suzuki.

The factory ran new twin-cylinders in the 125cc race but Degner was under-geared and could do not better than ▶

Suzuki SOUNDS OF THE SIXTIES

eighth, while Anderson went out when his machine's experimental crankshaft failed.

Although Itoh, the only Japanese rider to win a TT, and second-placed Anderson kept Suzuki in front during the 50cc race, the following year there was disappointment for Degner who went out at Waterworks on the final lap with ignition problems. Newcomer to the team, Isao Morishiro, and Ichino were fourth and fifth.

Suzuki's latest air-cooled, disc-valve 125 twins produced a claimed 25bhp and easily out-paced the Hondas. Anderson, Frank Perris and Degner filled the rostrum places, with Bertie Schneider taking fifth. Anderson's clear victory and a new lap record at 91.32mph came despite the fact that his machine was undergeared and over-jetted — and running some 200rpm under maximum.

Despite a renewed effort from Honda and Kreidler to knock Suzuki off the top of the 50cc championship, Anderson again ruled supreme as he won the 1964 TT race by over a minute with Morishita and Itoh, who was slowed with a sticking piston ring, third and fifth to claim the manufacturer's award.

It was disaster for the team in the 125 race, however, with all three of Suzuki's riders retiring early on. Although modified, the air-cooled machines had lost their edge and it wasn't until water-cooling was introduced later in the year that the situation started to improve for Suzuki. Things were just as glum in the 250 race when Perris, Anderson and Schneider all retired their new square-four, water-cooled, two-strokes that were fast but plagued by carburation problems and faults with the electronic ignition system for much of the season.

The 250, now with an eight-speed gearbox, was still not a competitive machine in 1965 and one of the only ray of hope for Suzuki came at the TT when Perris made third place ahead of Provini's factory Benelli.

Things were not all that bright in the 125cc race either. Anderson lost some ten seconds when he had to stop at the Guthrie Memorial on the first lap to change a plug on his water-cooled twin and, although he put in a new record lap at 96.02mph during a brilliant recovery charge, he was only fifth. Degner, also with plug fouling problems, was eighth, while Perris went out before Union Mills on the first lap.

The twin-cylinder, water-cooled, disc-valve 50cc machine had been completely re-vamped. It produced over 14bhp at 16,500rpm and had a 12-speed gearbox!

However, the new mount did prove good enough to beat Taveri's Honda in a weather-affected tiddler TT when carburation problems struck Anderson and Degner, forcing them to settle for second and third place. Itoh lost over a minute in the pits changing a plug.

By the end of the year Suzuki had dropped the troublesome 250, which was never seen again, so it was just the 50 and 125cc races that attracted the factory to the Island in 1966.

Hans-Georg Anscheidt, switched from Kreidler to Suzuki, and while he won the 50cc world crown, he failed to get further than Bray Hill on lap two of the TT when his twin, that had tightened on the Mountain, locked-up.

Anderson and Degner were third and fourth on the little Suzukis that now produced 16.5bhp and had 14-speed gearboxes.

Although he had a new short-stroke engine, Anderson was able to keep the Yamahas at bay in the 125 race when he finished third, with Perris fifth.

The following year was to be the final one of direct factory support from Suzuki with its most advance machine yet. It revved to over 17,000rpm, produced 17.5bhp and retained a 14-speed gearbox. After Itoh broke his wrist in practise and next in-line for honours, Yoshimi Katayama crashed while trying to make up ground after a first lap plug change, it was down to Stuart Graham to take his first TT win. Anscheidt, despite a misfire and oil leak, was second, and Robb on a production Suzuki, third.

Two years later, the class was restricted to machines with just one cylinder and six gears.

Graham, in second place, was the only Suzuki finisher in the 125cc race after Katayama's machine struck trouble at Sulby on lap one.

Later in the year Suzuki produced a new 90-degree, V-four 125 with disc inlet valves, geared crankshafts and water-cooling. But still the factory quit the GPs.

The 1965 50cc Suzuki works twin — water-cooled, disc-valve, 16,500rpm and 12-speed gearbox! (Mick Woollett Archive)

Suzuki 125cc works racer of 1963 with Degner-inspired disc valves. (Mick Woollett Archive)

The 1964 four-cylinder 250cc Suzuki RZ64: 54bhp at 12,000rpm with 26mm Mikunis, six-speed gearbox and thermo syphon cooling. The bike had little success due to persistent carburation and electronic ignition problems. (Mick Woollett Archive)

►

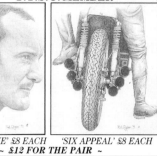

Yamaha SOUNDS OF THE SIXTIES

Yamaha's 250cc four of 1968. It was lighter and lower than the 1966 bike. Phil Read won the 250cc World Championship, ahead of team-mate Bill Ivy who won the Lightweight 250cc TT. (Mick Woollett Archive)

RD56 Yamaha 250cc twin of 1964. Read won the world title with the bike but had no luck at the TT. (Mick Woollett Archive)

Yamaha arrived quietly in 1961 — and in the wake of its high-flying rivals Honda, did a sound job in both the 250 and 125 races which failed to attract the attention it deserved.

Particularly impressive was Fumio Itoh, a newcomer to the TT. He took his massively-faired, twin-cylinder, two-stroke to an unheralded sixth place, and the last silver replica on offer, behind six Honda works men. He was there again in 11th place in the 125 race just ahead of one Hideo Oishi on a similar Yamaha. Although Yamaha then produced its first over-the-counter racer, the air-cooled, twin-cylinder TD1, the factory decided to give the 1962 European season a miss to re-assess its plans.

The TT was included in a three-meeting schedule for 1963 when Yamaha fielded an up-rated, 56mm x 50.7mm, disc-valve, air-cooled twin

that produced 47bhp at 12,5000rpm and featured a seven-speed gearbox.

Itch led on the first two laps of the Lightweight TT and continued to pressurise world champion Jim Redman during the remaining four and finally finishing second just a fraction over 17s behind the Honda rider. Tony Godfrey, on a similar Yamaha, crashed heavily near Milntown on the third lap after two stops for plug changes.

Phil Read became Yamaha's first 'foreign' rider signing for the 1964 season. Although the Englishman won the world title with the RD56 twin, there was little joy in store for him in the Island. He was fastest in practise for the Lightweight race and came within 2.2s of equalling Bob McIntyre's Honda-4 lap record, but problems with plugs ended his winning aspirations. Early on, Read was only 3.2 seconds down on Redman's Honda but then lost 1m 12s at the pits as he and a mechanic changed a plug apiece.

At the completion of the fourth lap, Read was in the lead by just over 8s but a further plug change was carried out when he stopped for fuel and from the re-start he got no further than Quarterbridge before the carburation problems ended his race.

Mike Duff, on a similar machine, stopped at Greeba Bridge on the first lap and Tommy Robb, on a third carburation-troubled Yamaha, pushed in from Governor's Bridge to take seventh, one place behind the private Yamaha of Roy Boughey.

Again there was no result for Yamaha in the 250 TT in 1965 when they returned with 30 bhp, disc-valve, nine-speed, water-cooled twins. With a standing start lap at over 100mph, Read was the race leader at the end of the first lap but then his engine seized at the Mountain Box. New signing, Bill Ivy, and Duff moved in to challenge Redman's lead but the former crashed while second on lap four when he tangled with a slower rider at Brandywell. Ivy pushed in, while Duff was over three seconds adrift at the finish.

Yamaha contested the 350 and 125 races for the first time that year and with a 250 over-bored to 254cc Read took the runner-up spot in the Junior and then won the smaller class event on a brand new water-cooled twin despite running on one cylinder from the Creg on the final lap. A similar problem befell third-placed Duff on the final lap, while Ivy, on a 1964 air-cooled twin, had to change a plug before making seventh place.

As competition grew in the smaller classes, Yamaha introduced four-cylinder, water-cooled machines for the 125 and 250cc events in 1966, but they were destined not to feature in the TT results that year.

Read and Ivy both ran 250cc fours, with two crankshafts geared together and with separate disc-valves for each cylinder. The machines were capable of around 160mph but it is not always speed that counts, as Read found out at Ginger Hall on lap two when a crankshaft broke while he was in second place.

Ivy fared little better. With the machine virtually running on only three cylinders; he changed a plug when he refuelled in third place at the end of lap four but got very little further before a cracked carburettor mounting proved to be the real reason for the problem.

Duff rode a twin but he too was in trouble right from the start, with a main bearing that finally collapsed at Appledene on lap two.

Yamaha decided to leave its four-cylinder 125 machines in the pits and instead sent its riders out on the well-proven twins in the Ultra Lightweight race. The decision was right — with Ivy and Read taking first and second places, and with Duff, suffering slight cramp, taking fifth to secure the manufacturer's award. A lower, lighter version of the 250-4, which by now was producing 70 bhp, was campaigned in the 250 race the following year. Read took the runner-up spot — the machine was no real match for Mike Hailwood's Honda. The luckless Ivy ended up pushing home with a broken crankshaft. Derek Chatterton headed the private Yamaha brigade in sixth place.

Honda had already pulled out of the 125 class so it was a two-stroke battle for supremacy between Suzuki and Yamaha which Read settled in Yamaha's favour by just under four seconds from Stuart Graham who headed the Suzuki onslaught.

Although Ivy's chances were dashed early on when his four became a three on the Mountain Climb, TT newcomer Akiyasu Motohashi, boosted the Yamaha effort with a third place. Yamaha was the only Japanese factory on the Isle of Man in 1968 — and that turned out to be its swansong! However, good spectator value was assured by a feud that had developed between Read and Ivy.

The 125-4 was now revving up to 18,000 and producing almost 46bhp. On one of these, 'little Bill' broke the 125 100mph barrier with a lap at 100.32mph. He led the race for four laps but on the final one slowed, under team orders, to let Read claim a controversial victory.

Ivy had already taken victory in the 250cc race on the larger four that produced some 70 bhp at just under 14,500rpm, after Read had gone out at the Bungalow on the fourth lap with a rear puncture.

Yamaha took the multis away at the end of the year because it considered further development of the disc-valve machine was no longer applicable to road-going machines. It marked the end of a glorious era that had seen all three Japanese manufacturers campaigning complex, exotic, new machinery at the TT. They could have asked for no greater test of their machines.

Words: *John Brown*

New Yamaha signing, Bill Ivy, at Ginger Hall on the 125cc in 1965. (Nick Nicholls)

This is the 1967 125cc Yamaha with water-cooled, two-stroke, four-cylinder engine and nine-speed gearbox. It revved to 15,400rpm and had a top speed of around 130mph. (Mick Woollett Archive)

Giacomo Agostini

Gla

Fine action study of Ago at Quarterbridge on the MV-3 during the 1971 TT. (Mick Woollett Archive)

Far Right: Senior TT winner's enclosure 1966 with Ago (left), Hailwood and Chris Conn. (Nick Nicholls)

Giacomo Agostini added a glamorous dimension to the attributes of TT hero-worshipping. The Italian's good looks and exciting personality made him an instant favourite with the female fans, and quite a few who had no interest whatsoever in the racing. He first stepped onto Isle of Man soil in 1965 and established himself among the elite during the years that followed.

"The girls, the fun, the socialising — it all went towards making the TT the most memorable event I ever contested," recalled Ago, who still lives in the small lake-side town of Bergamo in northern Italy. However, the handsome newcomer was quick to prove that he wasn't just a pretty face. By the time he quit racing on the Mountain Course, after claiming a victory double in 1972, he had amassed a total of ten wins — five each in the Junior and Senior races.

On his very first visit, Ago celebrated his 23rd birthday with third place in the 350cc race aboard an MV-3 when he partnered Mike Hailwood in the Italian team. Never lower than fifth on the leaderboard, he ended up racing on the road with second-placed Phil Read. With time on his side, the Yamaha rider actually waved the young Italian by as they headed down the Glencrutchery Road for the sixth and final time.

It was said by Read to be a birthday gesture, but it was a courtesy I don't think he would have repeated eight years later when the pair lived through a less tranquil time as riding partners

our Boy makes GOOD

1907

1917

1927

1937

1947

1957

1967

1977

1987

1997

in the MV team.

Things were not so bright for the newcomer two days later when he dropped his MV on the right hander at Sarah's Cottage during the second lap of a wet and windy Senior. He was uninjured, but unable to continue on the damaged multi.

While he was sitting it out on the following lap, Ago got the shock of his life when team-mate Hailwood landed at his feet after being caught by the same slippery patch of road. The British rider, however, was able to continue on his battered machine and took centre spot on the winner's rostrum.

However, Ago had done enough to prove his worth, for not only had he made the rostrum in the Junior and held second place at the end of the first lap of the Senior, but he had headed the practice leaderboard during the early part of the week and set the best time during a very wet session on Friday.

"I took the TT challenge very seriously," said Ago. "I went to the Isle of Man a few weeks before the TT to find my way round the circuit. I must have done well over 50 laps in a car and on a

motorbike before practise started. It was all very exciting for me that year. I was young and brave and had been told that I was going to race on a circuit that was unlike anything I had experienced before.

"When I saw the long straights, the ups and downs, the change of road surface and all the things that lined the circuit like telegraph poles, walls, kerbs — and even telephone boxes — I couldn't believe that I was actually there to race a motorcycle. And it was so long; I thought it would be impossible for me to find my way round at racing speeds.

"It was to be a challenge that I was determined to master and, as I have said so many times before, I think that for actual riding and rider satisfaction it is the best circuit in the world.

"But it is dangerous. If you crash, the chances of getting hurt are high and when I started losing friends like Gilberto Parlotti, who was killed there in 1972, I decided I just had to stop riding in the TT.

"I can understand why riders today still want to race there and I think the good thing now is that because the event is not part of a championship it is down to personal choice. There are no team pressures to make a rider take part."

Ago still happily reminisces about his years of TT racing, about the atmosphere — everything which he found so enjoyable. He also talks with fondness of his visits to the Island in recent years, with racing no longer on his schedule.

Even after all his racing exploits, and the high and lows he experienced during a career that brought a record 15 world titles, Ago always recalls the day in 1967 when a broken chain robbed him of a victory that to him would have been greater than all the 122 grand prix wins he secured.

Giacomo Agostini *Glamour Boy makes good*

Roll the camera's, Ago's here!
The fans crane forward to see
their hero during the 1966
Junior. (Mick Woollett Archive)

It was the clash of the titans — Ago on the MV and Hailwood on the Honda — and the crowds had flocked to the Island. For the first four laps the Italian held a slender advantage and on the opening one became the first rider to crack the 21-minute barrier with a speed of 108.38mph.

But as he rounded Windy Corner on the penultimate lap, the rear chain of the MV broke. Although his chances were fast fading, Ago coasted and pushed his way back to the pits where his mechanics were waiting with a replacement chain, but to no avail because the sprocket was wrecked. For a tearful Ago the race was over.

"I knew I could win and even Mike knew that too," said Ago. "The first thing he did after winning was to come over to me, put his hand on a shoulder and say, 'It was yours today, you should be the one getting the winner's applause'."

What Ago only confessed when I was speaking with him recently was that amidst the deep disappointment and tears there was a bright spot during the night that followed the race.

"The girl friend I had that year had not been too receptive to my advances until that evening," he explained as a broad grin broke across his face. "I think she felt sorry for me, it was wonderful."

Agostini's first victory came in 1966 when, as the first Italian to win the Junior TT, he had some ten minutes and almost 15 miles of road in hand over second-placed Peter Williams, a newcomer to the Course that year, on Tom Arter's AJS.

The Hailwood threat disappeared with Honda magneto failure on the lap and Ago romped around on his own, topping the 100mph mark on every lap, except the third when he re-fuelled. He smashed the lap record, leaving it at 103.09mph, "just for fun," on the second after he had seen a stranded Hailwood at Bishopscourt.

However, he had to settle for second behind 'Mike the Bike' in the Senior when the British rider's Honda and his MV were separated by over 2.5 minutes.

With a seemingly endless trail of broken-down bikes in his wake — 48 of the 85 starters including the rest of the leaderboard favourites all fell by the wayside — Agostini got his first Senior win in 1968. After his team-mate for the event, John Hartle, crashed at Cronk-ny-Mona on the first lap, Agostini cruised around to a victory of over eight minutes from Seeley-mounted Brian Ball.

It was the first year that Agostini clinched a Junior/Senior double victory and, as rival factory support dwindled, he achieved the same results every year until he called it a day in 1972 — except in 1971 when the unbelievable happened and the 350 MV struck engine trouble at Ramsey on the first lap. There were cheers from the crowd, who sensed a close battle now that the dominate multi was sidelined, and there was a hero's welcome for Tony Jefferies when he took his Yamsel to victory.

It was a period when Ago dominated the world with little opposition and it was not a time that over-excited him.

"I much preferred to have a close race when it was an achievement to win," he said. "Those early battles at the TT were among the most enjoyable times in my racing career. If you mastered the Mountain Course you were a true racer. When I was young the danger issue didn't not bother me too much, but as I got older I felt that a rider should have chance of escaping injury if he crashed and that was not possible at so many places in the Island."

After losing his close friend Parlotti, who he showed round the Course the evening before his death in the 125 race, Ago admits that it did take a lot of persuasion to get him to race in the following Senior TT.

"I was ready to go home, I had no real enthusiasm for the race, but it had to be done because I was a professional rider in a world championship team," he said. He won his final race in commanding style from MV team-mate Alberto Pagani who inherited second place on the final lap when Peter Williams went out at the Bungalow. Earlier in the week Ago dominated the Junior, after Phil Read (on a second MV) retired on the second lap.

Ago stood by his decision never to race in the TT again but just the same he still admits that the Isle of Man was where he enjoyed some of his most memorable and enjoyable conquests, both on and off the track!

Words: *John Brown*

One that got away. The unthinkable happened during the 1971 Junior when Ago's MV quit. (Nick Nicholls)

TT Gallery 1907-1949

1909

Harry Reed (left) is away first on his Dot Peugeot ahead of Jack Marshall's Triumph at the start of the 1909 TT. (Mick Woollett Archive)

1909

Early TT — on the St John's short circuit. Eric Myers, on a twin-cylinder two-stroke Scott, passes a broken down machine during the 1909 TT. Myers later crashed on the seventh lap and retired. (Mick Woollett Archive)

1926

S Jackson approaches Hillberry on his HRD Jap during the 1926 Senior TT. He finished eighth. (Mick Woollett Archive)

1913

For the 1913 TT the finish line was at the bottom of Bray Hill. Scott-mounted H O Wood crosses the line to win the Senior at the same spot where Ago would later fly the MV Agusta! (Mick Woollett Archive)

1948

Artie Bell, pictured at Quarterbridge, went on to finish third in the 1948 Junior TT. The Norton rider was beaten by Velocette men Freddie Frith and Bob Foster. Bell had his moment of glory, however, winning the Senior race after finishing runner-up the previous year. (Mick Woollett Archive)

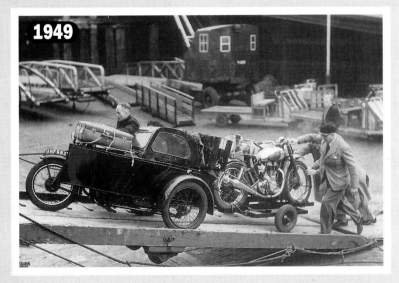

1949

The way we were — or at least 'the way we used to travel'. Sidecar for wife and child, trailer with two solos... plus the cases strapped on fore and aft. TT enthusiast boards the ferry at Liverpool Docks. (Mick Woollett Archive)

1947

Senior TT, 1947, 'weigh in'... with Jock West's 500 AJS Porcupine (45) and Bob Foster's Velocette (46) under close scrutiny. (Mick Woollett Archive)

TT Gallery 1949-1958

In 1949, the Duke of Edinburgh (pictured second left) started the Senior TT, then watched some of the racing from this spot at the Creg-Ny-Baa Hotel with Professor A M Low (left) of the ACU. (Mick Woollett Archive)

1949

Arthur Wheeler finished eighth on this dust-bin-faired 250 Moto Guzzi in the 1957 250 TT which was held on the Clypse Course. (Nick Nicholls)

1957

Typical Liverpool scene from the early post-war years as enthusiasts queue on the dockside for a ferry to the Isle of Man. (Mick Woollett Archive)

1949

1950

Guy Newman bumps his 'Velo' into life at the start of the 1950 Junior TT. Waiting in line are Dickie Dale (AJS No4), J Boardman (Norton No6), Aussie Eric McPherson (AJS No6), Bill Storr (AJS No9) and Crommie McCandless (Norton 11). Artie Bell won the race on a Norton. (Mick Woollett Archive)

1958

Manx Arms, Onchan on the Clypse course - Ernst Degner finished fifth on this 125cc MZ in the Ultra-light-weight race. (Nick Nicholls)

Renzo Pasolini powers the works Benelli around Quarterbridge during the 1968 Junior TT. He finished runner-up to Giacomo Agostini and the MV. Pasolini also finished second in the 250 Lightweight race. Bill Ivy

1968

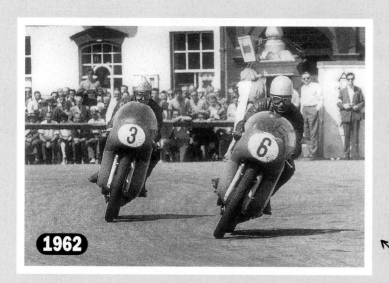

1962

Another Junior TT, this time in 1962, in what has been described as one of the finest post-war TT races. Gary Hocking leads Mike Hailwood at Parliament Square. Hailwood won the titanic duel by five seconds. (Nick Nicholls)

1960

Flyin' high. John Hartle won the 1960 Junior TT at a new race record average of 96.70mph on the MV Agusta but second placed team-mate, John Surtees, had the consolation of setting a new lap record at 99.20mph (Nick Nicholls)

The 50cc 'tiddlers' entertained at the TT in the 1960s. Start line during the 1962 race sees Dan Shorey astride a Kreidler with Mitsuo Itoh (12) getting his Suzuki under way. Ernst Degner won the race. Itoh would have to wait until the following year to become the first Japanese rider to win a TT. (Nick Nicholls)

1962

TT Gallery 1969-1996

1973

Peter Williams scored the first TT win for the John Player Norton team in the 1973 Formula 750 TT. (Nick Nicholls)

1970s

Mick Grant won three TTs on Kawasakis; the '75 Senior, the '77 and '78 Classics. In the latter two he also set new race and lap records. (Don Morley)

1994

TT racing in the 1990s. Down on his knee and hard on the gas, it's Steve Hislop in full flight on a Castrol Honda in 1994. After a two-year absence from the event, he dominated TTF1 and Senior races with race speeds over 119mph and a fastest lap in the Senior of 122.50mph. He hasn't been back since. (Terry Howe)

1996

Dave Molyneux and Pete Hill set new standards during their 1996 Sidecar TT double win, lapping at 111.02mph in the Wednesday's race and averaging 110.28mph for the three-lapper. (Terry Howe)

Alan Barnett upheld British honour in the 1969 Junior TT, by finishing runner-up to MV's Giacomo Agostini. This picture was taken during the Junior TT, with Barnett on Tom Kirby's Metisse at Ramsey Hairpin. (Nick Nicholls)

1973

1960

Helmut Fath only won one Sidecar TT, in 1960, but was a force to be reckoned with in the sport right through the decade. With Wolfgang Kalauch, seen here along the Glencrutchery Road, he finished fourth in the 1968 500 Sidecar TT with the URS500. (Nick Nicholls)

1962

The 1962 season was a memorable one in Sidecar racing history with Chris Vincent and Eric Bliss beating the German favourites with this BSA-powered outfit. To complete a great year for the Brits, Colin Seeley finished third on his Matchless.

1974

Mac Hobson powers the unsilenced Ham Yam through Sulby Bridge. The Hobson/Armstrong partnership finished fourth in the 500 Sidecar TT of 1974. Hobson won two TTs but, along with passenger Kenny Birch, was killed in a crash at Bray Hill just after the start of Monday's race in 1978. (Nick Nicholls)

1963

1967

High-speed traffic in the 1963 Sidecar TT at Ginger Hall with Owen Greenwood/Terry Fairbrother (Matchless) leading Charlie Freeman /Billie Nelson (Norton) and third-place finishers Alan and Peter Birch (BMW). Greenwood finished eighth. Freeman retired. (Nick Nicholls)

Schauzu and Schneider, pictured at the Gooseneck on their BMW, won the Sidecar TT in 1967. Enders and Seeley completed the podium. (Nick Nicholls)

Mike Hailwood

Mike Hailwood won 14 TTs in a Mountain Course career that continued through until 1979 when a well-timed comeback helped boost the event's flagging fortunes.

Glorious comeback! Hailwood won the TT Formula One race at record-breaking speeds in 1978 riding a Ducati. He upped the race average to 108.51mph and the lap record to 110.62mph. (Nick Nicholls)

Mike Hailwood will long remain a true legend of TT racing in the Isle of Man. His total of 14 victories has only been surpassed by Joey Dunlop, and in 1961 he was the first rider to win three races in a week — a milestone he would have been the first to admit was tinged with more than a fair amount of luck.

A promised factory 125 Honda failed to materialise and he settled for the machine Luigi Taveri had used in practise for the Ultra-Lightweight race. Mike beat the Italian by just two seconds, despite battling against a lack of power and risking everything on the corners.

He was in a no-hope situation with a Honda-4 in the Lightweight race, behind favourites Bob McIntyre on a Honda and Gary Hocking on an MV. However, Hocking retired on lap two with engine problems and when Mac's Honda seized on the final lap, Hailwood was the winner.

The Senior was even more of a sensation, when he took a 500 Norton to victory for the final time on the Island behind Hocking's troublesome 'private' MV-4. He kept up so much pressure on the ailing multi that Hocking took to the slip road at Ballacraine and handed the British rider precious seconds.

It could well have been four wins for Mike that year, if a gudgeon pin in his AJS had not broken with less than half a lap of the Junior remaining, while he was almost three minutes in the lead following the expiry of Hocking's MV.

There is no doubt that a large number of Hailwood's outstanding performances were delivered at the Island.

Post-1961 Senior with Hailwood celebrating victory. Left to right: Tom Phillis (third place), Pamela Lawton, Mike Hailwood, Stan Hailwood, Bob McIntyre and a pensive Reg Armstrong. (Nick Nicholls)

Mounta

in Maestro

Tourist Trophy

1907

1917

1927

1937

1947

1957

1967

1977

1987

1997

Mike Hailwood Mountain Maestro

They spanned two decades from the time he was a teenage newcomer to the sensational come-back years of the late 1970s when he proved there is no real substitute for experience when it comes to mastering the rigours of the Mountain Course.

Mike was just 19 when he arrived on the Isle of Man for his second TT outing in 1959 with only two years' racing behind him, to mix-it with the world's best 250 riders in the Lightweight TT that was being run on the Clypse Circuit for the final time.

He lined up on the Glencrutchery Road for the massed start with an eight-year-old privately-owned Mondial alongside the likes of grand prix-experienced riders Carlo Ubbiali and Tarquinio Provini on factory MVs.

No one really gave him a chance of keeping up the pace with the world title-chasing Italians and their rivals on the grand prix scene.

However, the young lad from Oxfordshire was about to turn on sensational performance number one. At the end of the first lap he was on the tail of the two leading MVs and there he stayed for the next two, before

sweeping past the pair of them, to lead the race as they flashed past the Grandstand at the end of lap five.

Mike was still there at the end of the sixth, but then on the next he was out of the contest when the Mondial's ignition expired. Whilst this was not a race for the official record books, it still had that stamp of true greatness!

Similar stories of bad luck came in 1962 when an already established TT-riding Mike was on a last-minute hunt for 125 and 250 rides to back up those already made for him by Honda in the Senior and Junior events.

Earlier in the season Mike had raced one of Dr Joe Ehrlich's 125 EMCs in Spain, where he gave an inspired show until the expansion chamber of the two-stroke split — so Dr Joe offered him the machine for a second time.

Despite some poor handling characteristics, that even a new frame failed to banish, Mike used the excellent power of the machine to split the all-conquering four-stroke Hondas right up until the final lap when the hard-pressed two-stroke cried "enough".

More Hailwood heroics came in the 250 race when he accepted an offer from Fron Purslow to race an elderly single-cylinder Benelli, because a promised four-cylinder machine from the same factory had failed to materialise.

Although Purslow, a racer himself, was among the leaders of the time when it came to the technical side of the sport, he was not renowned for the finer points of machine preparation, and this did rather show when Mike set off in the opening practise. However, he was firmly among the front runners by race day and got in with the fancied factory riders right from the start. For the first two laps the private Benelli was in fourth, but at the end of the third, Mike rode into the pits with the fairing hanging off the sorry-looking Italian single.

Of course there was no giving up for the eager pilot who, with assistance from Fron, ripped off the offending fibreglass and hurtled back into the race, naked and unashamed, minus screen and numbers.

He battled on, lacking speed and out of the running until the penultimate lap when the over-worked engine, that had produced a 92mph second lap, packed-up.

Not all the great rides ended in failure of course, and one of his best efforts was his victory ride in the 1965 Senior. In appalling conditions he crashed at Sarah's Cottage while leading on a works MV and literally kicked the damaged multi back into shape so that he

1907

1917

1927

1937

1947

1957

1967

1977

1987

1997

could nurse it back to the pits, some 27 miles away, where alerted mechanics could carry out a check.

He went back out for the last tension-packed lap with a shattered screen and with one of the four cylinders attempting to run flat-out because the pit crew had removed a throttle slide to overcome the problem of a stone that had jammed in the carburettor during the incident.

The previous year, Mike had raced against the course doctor's advice and won the Senior for MV. A heavy dose of flu had left him in a weak condition, sidelined him from the Junior, and he was almost 10lbs underweight when he pushed the four-cylinder machine onto the start-line. It was one of the many occasions when Mike raced against the odds, a situation that never failed to bring out the brilliant best in him.

To say he looked shattered when he arrived in the finishers' enclosure would be an understatement, but he was the victor by over three minutes from Norton-riding Derek Minter.

Another sterling Hailwood performance that ended without a result came in 1965, when he raced the virtually untried three-cylinder 350 MV in the Junior race. His only previous experience of the triple was at the West German GP earlier in the year when it packed up after a few laps of practise and he was forced to revert to the older four-cylinder machine for the race.

On the Isle of Man, Mike only managed to complete three laps on the triple during the practise week. The handling was atrocious and to make matters worse, the final practise session was run in the wet when it was impossible for him to find out if the modifications made to the machine worked.

Before the weigh-in the MV mechanics attempted a last-gasp effort to make the bike steer by utilising various parts from other machines, including the forks and rear shock absorbers from the 500cc example.

In the race he faced Jim Redman and the Honda-4, a combination that had proved to be unbeatable during the previous two Juniors and which was well fancied to make it three in a row.

From a slowish start, the amazing Hailwood set about hammering the predictions of the experts by closing in on Redman, taking the lead over the Mountain and ending the first lap with a 20s advantage on what in truth was a 'hack'.

However, the gallant effort ended at the end of the next lap when he pulled into the pits with an oil-covered engine and a well-stretched chain. Just the same, he proved yet again that he was the master of the world's toughest race — against the odds.

From Greeba Bridge on a very hot Wednesday in June 1962, I watched a classic Hailwood performance in the Junior race when both he and the late Gary Hocking were astride near identical MV-4s.

It was obviously a race of tactics because one of them was set to be the winner. Mike had the disadvantage of starting 10s before the Rhodesian which meant he either had to try to pile on the speed to increase this margin and risk blowing up the motor or let his rival catch him and go for victory in the closing stages.

Hailwood chose the latter, letting Hocking go into the lead on the road and then staying with him until the fifth lap when he made a break. This of course meant that there was the marvellous sight and sound of the two MVs as they screamed round the island and the excitement at the pits when they refuelled together.

Mike made his effort coming down the Mountain and made up five seconds on the penultimate lap — he then set about extending this to seven on the last one, to snatch two seconds' win on corrected time.

It was all going according to plan until a few miles from home when Mike's bike started to misfire on the final Mountain climb. Luckily for him, a similar bug attacked Hocking's multi, so he managed to ease over the line with a five-second advantage.

Hocking got his revenge two days later in the Senior when Mike started 30s behind his team-mate but then lost almost a quarter of an hour in the pits sorting out a clutch problem.

Heroic rides in the Senior followed, when Mike switched from MV to Honda in 1966. It was simply awesome, watching him battle round from kerb-to-kerb or verge-to-verge on the four-cylinder Honda that he rated as the worst handling machine he had ever ridden. However, the first clash to be witnessed by British race fans between Mike on the Honda-4 and Agostini on the MV was a record breaking affair for both contestants. It was Mike's lap record at 107.07mph on the third lap that was to clinch the deal.

Hailwood had a lucky win in 1967 when the chain of Ago's MV broke on the fifth Mountain descent and brought one of the greatest TT battles ever to an untimely conclusion.

Only seconds had separated the pair as they shared the lead, even on the fateful fifth lap by which time Mike was having to hold the throttle twist grip on the handlebars because attempts to

Hailwood on his way to one of three TT race wins during 1961 — this is during the Senior at Signpost Corner on a Manx Norton. (Nick Nicholls)

Tourist Trophy

Mike Hailwood Mountain Maestro

1907

1917

1927

1937

1947

1957

1967

1977

1987

1997

tighten it with a hammer during his pit stop had failed.

At the Bungalow, Ago was just over two seconds in the lead, but then disaster struck for the Italian. Hailwood was on his way to a 12th TT victory, that he personally regarded as lucky, in what was scheduled to be his final race on the Mountain Course.

He had won three races in a week for a second time and with Honda pulling out of racing at the end of the year, Hailwood turned his attention to Formula 5000 and then Formula One car racing.

When the TT lost its Grand Prix World Championship status, and the big names of motorcycle racing turned their backs on the Isle of Man there was a void that some predicated would threaten the very future of the event.

Fortunately, just when it needed it the most, the TT got the greatest boost it could have hoped for — the return of 'Mike the Bike'.

In 1978 — thanks mainly to the efforts of 'Daily Mirror' sports writer Ted Macauley — 35-year-old Hailwood returned to the Island to race once more.

The fans headed back in their thousands, not only to see their hero race again but also to see him confront his old adversary, Phil Read.

Read, winner of the Formula One race the previous year when he was on a comeback trip, was there to defend his victory with a factory-prepared Honda. For the mighty confrontation Mike had a Ducati, not a full works one as originally planned, but an example prepared and entered by Sports Motorcycles boss Steve Wynne. Steve had picked up the loose ends when factory officials said they could not arrange insurance cover for Hailwood and withdrew their support. With the Ducati, Hailwood's much-heralded return started in fairytale fashion as he romped to victory in the Formula One race after passing Read on the road, who then went out when his big money Honda expired at the 11th Milestone on the penultimate lap.

However, the rest of the week proved to be an anti-climax. Although Martini, sponsors for Hailwood's return, produced the razzmatazz, Yamaha — who provided the bikes — seemed to be lacking in urgency and preparation for an event that they did not seem to be taking seriously enough. Mike was fit and geared up to give his adoring fans full value for money but the Yamahas could not live up to the moment.

In the Senior, run on Monday, the steering-damper broke while he was running third at Ramsey and after work at the pits he made 28th place. Hailwood didn't fancy his chances in Wednesday's Lightweight race — he was looking on it as extra practise for the Classic race clash with Mick Grant two days later. He had to make one fuel stop more than everyone else because the tank was too small and finished 12th. Then his attack on the Classic ended on the first lap when his Yamaha's crankshaft broke. He shared the disappointment of the fans and before leaving the Island vowed he would be back the following year to make amends.

From the Isle of Man in 1978 Mike went to Mallory Park for the Post TT meeting and produced what I still regard as the most memorable and sensational performance of his magical come-back. With the very same TT-winning Ducati, Mike beat the best of the short circuit riders including Read, and without a rear brake.

As promised he went back to the Island in 1979, this time with a factory Ducati backed by Sports Motorcycles (a shadow of its private equivalent the previous year), and Senior and Classic race 500cc machines provided by Suzuki GB. Mike never thought he had a chance in the F1 — indeed it was won by Alex George who had taken over the Honda entry from injured Mick Grant. In the end he was fifth on an over-revving Ducati that shook off its battery at Hillberry on the last lap and resulted in its rider having to effect some re-wiring before performing an uphill bump-start to get back in the race. Mike's 14th and final TT victory came in Wednesday's Senior race with a lap and race record-breaking display on the Suzuki that saw him well clear of second-placed Tony Rutter. This was followed by another epic battle in the Classic, when he pitted the 500 Suzuki against the mighty 998cc Honda Britain machine that Ron Haslam had taken to third place in the F1 race.

It was another race that looked as though Mike was going to win as he headed through Ramsey for the sixth and final time with a slender lead over his Scottish challenger. A superhuman effort over the Mountain by George, however, gave him the verdict by 3.4s and record race average of 113.08mph — not bad for 18 years ago!

Mike was tragically killed in a road accident, for which he was blameless, while driving his children to a fish and chip shop near his home on March 21, 1981. To his race fans worldwide he lives on as a legend, and nowhere more so than at the Isle of Man.

Words: *John Brown*

Braddan Bridge, Senior TT 1965: Mike Hailwood battles on with a bloody nose and an MV with a smashed screen. (Nick Nicholls)

'In Pursuit of Perfection' is the title of Duke's autobiography. It says much about a dogged approach to racing that made him one of the greatest stars the sport has ever known.

1907

1917

1927

1937

1947

1957

1967

1977

1987

1997

Geoff Duke single-minded disposition

Previous Page: Singles back on top. Norton's new 'featherbed' models took a Senior 1-2-3 in 1950. Winner Duke (centre) is congratulated by third man, Johnny Lockett (49) and Artie Bell (41). Norton boss Gilbert Smith (hat) and Joe Craig look on. (Mick Woollett Archive)

Right: Geoff Duke faces the starter for the 1952 Senior — his last race as a works Norton rider before joining Gilera in 1953. (Mick Woollett Archive)

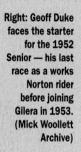

"It was the ultimate! Whether mechanically, physically or mentally, the TT was the ultimate challenge. It was in my day, and I believe that even today, while the world's Grand Prix stars won't race there, it still remains a dream for a lot of our country's top riders."

Ultimate challenge. While the words of the opening paragraph echo a modern day TT sound-bite, you sit back and take notice when they come from the mouth of Geoff Duke.

The man is a legend in motorcycle racing history. Five world titles and six TT wins, yet Duke also had a reputation as a single-minded individual who didn't suffer fools gladly.

Now into his seventies — but looking a good 20 years younger — he nevertheless displays a charm that makes for an absorbing interview.

TT legend would have it that Duke had the TT in his blood from being a young boy back in St Helens, but he refutes this.

"I always had motorcycles around me from about 12 years of age. My brother raced, so it was in the family blood I think," he says. "I was always aware of the TT, and I remember following Jimmy Simpson's exploits quite closely in the 1920s, via Graham Walker's radio commentaries. But I never harboured any great ambitions to race on the Isle of Man — or anywhere else for that matter.

"I didn't actually start competition riding until after the Second World War [as a dispatch rider instructor]. After I was demobbed I got a job at BSA as a trials rider. I had learned trials riding from my Sergeant, Hugh Viney — a top-class trials rider of the era — during the war.

"I did quite well, with BSA and the next year Artie Bell asked me to join the Norton trials team — by which time I had developed an interest in road racing. I was aware of the TT Course and its reputation so that seemed like the best place to start! Initially I was going to enter the 1948 Clubmans TT but the entries were over-subscribed, so I went to the Manx instead.

"Norton loaned me a standard bike for the Junior. I remember at the start — I had number 12 — feeling absolutely fantastic. I had a couple of chaps signalling for me — but all they could give me were lap times. However, I could see on the second lap that I was already lapping three minutes quicker than I had in practise."

During Duke's pit stop at the end of the third lap, his pit helper refused to tell him he was placed second in case he started to push too hard. After the pit stop the race started to go awry for Geoff.

"I had two almighty slides on the fourth lap, one at Braddan, then at Ballacraine. I took it a bit easy until

ing the lap record too.

"I'd been a bit surprised by the speed of Artie's 350 in the Junior", Duke recalls. "It was very rapid for a Norton — against the Velocettes and AJSs of the time anyhow. I finished second, which was quite pleasing, but we never did find out why Artie's bike was so much quicker. It was just one of those things. Mind you, I probably had the quickest of the 500s for the Senior."

Duke claims that he actually wasn't surprised to win a TT in his first year, well not as surprised as he had been at leading that 1948 Manx Grand Prix anyway! He admits, however, that part of his TT triumph was down to former winner Harold Daniell. Duke explains: "I had watched the 1949 TT on the Mountain above Windy Corner where there is a series of three fast left-hand bends [Brandywell]. Basically to be fast through this section you needed to take the bends in one sweep. I watched Daniell win the Senior TT that year and he was absolutely flat out — about 120mph — taking the bends on the same immaculate line, every lap. It was fantastic. For the first, and only, time in my racing career I made a conscientious effort to copy another rider rather than go with my own style."

Returning in 1951, Duke won what was surprisingly his only TT Junior/Senior double. He was supremely confident at the time.

"Looking back, I would say that I was at the height of my racing powers then", he says. "I had quite a bit of experience behind me, and I still had a fair bit of dash about me — that's to say I hadn't scared myself to death yet. So I was confident I had the ability, and by the time of the TT, the bikes too."

The 350cc Norton prior to the TT had experienced numerous problems in the first two world championship rounds of 1951. However, after the bike was stripped following the Swiss GP just before the Isle of Man event, Norton identified problems with spark plugs and the magneto with the help of the legendary Polish engineer Cosmicky.

"The bike was completely transformed. Even on the first lap of practise I knew it was a different bike. So different, that I had a very hairy moment at Laurel Bank — just by going too quickly. Obviously that was a lesson learnt and in the race we decimated the field — and the lap record too."

It was the first lap over 90mph by a 350cc, and for good measure Geoff upped his own 500cc lap record during an easy Senior win.

"I would have been disappointed not to have won the Senior because the bike was the best out there. The Gileras were staying away, so there was really only my team-mates to beat,

Ramsey where the thing seemed a little bit more stable and I gave it a go up the Mountain. About three quarters of the way up the Mountain Mile, the engine seized. I remember strolling up to the Mountain Box and a marshal asked me who I was and what had happened? So I told him. 'Pity', he said. 'You were leading'."

Far from being downcast, Duke was pleased. Remember, this was his first major road race — and on the Mountain Course to boot. He returned in 1949, firstly to win the Clubmans TT and then later that year he duly beat hot favourite Cromie McCandless to win the Senior Manx Grand Prix. By 1950 he was in the 'works' Norton team.

By TT time Duke had pioneered the one-piece racing leathers. He was also becoming a very useful racer. He finished second to Artie Bell in the Junior, but won the Senior ahead of teammates, Bell and Johnny Lockett, break-

and I was confident in my own ability."

After winning the 350 and 500cc World Championship titles in 1951, the following year was a significant one in Duke's racing career. He encountered mixed fortunes both at World Championship level and at the TT. He won the Junior TT at a canter from Rod Coleman's AJS. However, Duke seemingly had the Senior TT in the bag before the Norton failed, allowing team-mate, Reg Armstrong, to win.

"The 1952 500 wasn't as good as the 1951 model, but it was still okay for the TT. I was leading the race comfortably — by 28s or so — on the third lap when the clutch failed. I got back to the pits to re-fuel, but couldn't get it started again."

An accident in Germany at Schotten during a non-championship race cost him a broken ankle and the 500cc World Championship (although he had already retained his 350cc title).

Despite this he was awarded the OBE and voted 'Sportsman of the Year'. Yet the accident had a profound effect on Duke, which ultimately resulted in him 'defecting' to Gilera for the 1953 season, but the deal was clinched very late in the day, and his first major race on the Italian machine was to be the 1953 Senior TT.

"I'd run the bike briefly at Monza and had been immediately impressed with the engine, which was very smooth and silky", Duke explains. "The handling and gearbox, however, left a lot to be desired, and while we sorted out the majority of the gearbox problems by the time of the TT, the handling did have me a little concerned."

Duke did 13 laps in practise, none of which was a flyer, as he tried to sort out the troublesome suspension. By race time the team felt they had made some progress and Duke duly set the early pace. Then on the third lap, after he had passed his main protagonist Ray Amm on the 'works' Norton, the gearbox gremlins returned, allowing the Rhodesian back in front.

"I quickly caught Ray up on the road again and decided to follow him for a while, which was exciting to say the least," continues Duke. "It was one of the scariest things I've ever done. To say his riding was lurid would be an understatement."

Duke stopped for fuel at the end of the third lap, but Amm was planning to go through the seven-lap race non-stop, his Norton being fitted with pannier fuel tanks. Duke, however, remained confident.

"I knew he had been on the edge keeping up with me, as he had to slipstream", he explains. "So I knew that if I could catch him reasonably quickly and get rid of him on the road I'd be in

1907

1917

1927

1937

1947

1957

1967

1977

1987

1997

Geoff Duke *single-minded disposition*

Above: In 1951 Duke won both the Senior and Junior TTs. The works Norton rider closes in on Tommy McEwan's Norton at Governor's. (Mick Woollett Archive)

Right: Duke walks back to the paddock with race official Norman Brown after winning the 1951 Senior aboard a works Norton. (Mick Woollett Archive)

with a chance. I set off down Bray Hill on the fourth lap, really winding it on — coming down to Quarterbridge the bike went into a slide [the road had recently been re-surfaced, and on this a very hot day, tar had risen to the surface and the tyres just slipped away]. When this happened on the Norton I would shut the throttle off and the engine would just die away gradually, but on the Gilera the power shut-down was sudden and the tyres gripped again and I was thrown off. I wasn't hurt but I couldn't restart the bike because the alloy tank had been ground away in the accident and fuel was leaking out."

Duke would have obviously loved to have beaten his old Norton team first time out, but the ultimate revenge would be his as he went on to win the World Championship in his first season for Gilera.

Controversy was never too far from Geoff Duke, whether it was his departure from Norton, or supporting the privateers' strike at Assen in 1955, and in-between there had been an incident at the 1954 TT where Duke and the racing authorities again crossed swords. Geoff explains.

"The 1954 Senior was the best chance I ever had to win a race before it had even started. Over the preceding winter Gilera completely redesigned the motorcycle — of which my input had

been influential. It was an absolutely superb machine — it didn't need a steering damper, even round here [the Isle of Man]. The reason for that was mainly the weight distribution, which was all on the front wheel — around 60%, although the geometry remained similar to the Norton. There is no doubt in my mind that the bike would have lapped at over 100mph. It was much better than the '55 bike. In the end though, the race should never have been started."

Race day conditions were abysmal and in Duke's opinion the race authorities unnecessarily risked the riders' lives.

"The thing I never forgave the ACU for was their decision to stop the race at the end of the fourth lap — even

though they had met as early as the second lap to decide what to do. The reason they left it until lap four was so that the race would count for World Championship points. They completely ignored the fact that they were putting everyone at risk. In fact by lap four the conditions were improving, and the weather on the Mountain was acceptable, and when I completed that fourth lap the sun was shining, but by then I had refuelled and the race was stopped [and Ray Amm going non-stop -again — had won]. My race engineer had timed the fourth lap from the top of Bray Hill and my lap time had improved by 28s. The pit stop cost me a minute or so, and ultimately, the race."

Duke finally won a TT for Gilera at the third time of asking in 1955. However, his victory seems destined to be overshadowed in TT folklore by the fact that he just missed out on the first ever 100mph lap.

"Yes, it was 40 minutes before they corrected the time, but really I wasn't too disappointed, I was just so pleased that I had finally won here for Gilera", explains Duke. "Old Man Gilera was at the TT that year and he was over the moon; he had so desperately wanted a TT win.

"It would have been nice to have the 100mph lap, and to be fair even if they had made a slight error, and let's face it, it was all hand timed, it would have paid them [the organisers] to let the time stand."

Although Duke remained with Gilera for another two seasons he missed the 1956 and 1957 TTs; the former due to his role in the previously mentioned riders' strike of 1955, for which he, amongst others, was banned for six months. And in 1957 he was injured for most of the season — the year Bob McIntyre achieved the first 100mph TT lap. Following Gilera's withdrawal, Duke rode privately-entered machines in 1958 and 1959 (he finished a creditable fourth in the 1959 Junior — aboard a Norton) and retired gracefully.

Duke will remain a TT legend for as long as motorcycles are raced on the Isle of Man, and the place has kept its hold on him too. He has lived on the Island for many years now and enjoyed business success since his racing interests have stopped. He now lives close to the TT course in happy retirement.

Duke's recall of races, people, technical issues, and even his detail of remote test sessions is impressive and there is still evidence of that single-minded attitude that ultimately made him one of the most successful riders of all time.

1907
1917
1927
1937
1947
1957
1967
1977
1987
1997

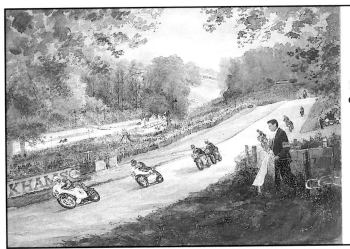

TT Chronicle

1907-1997

1909

1922

1906

The Auto Cycle Club (the fore-runner to the ACU) decides on a requirement to send a strong British representation to the International Cup races in Austria. They agree the necessity of trials to ascertain the quickest riders and bikes. Because of British mainland restrictions preventing any motor vehicle from travelling at over 20mph, the ACC accepts the Manx Government's invitation to hold the 'trials' on public roads — where no speed restrictions are imposed and the roads can be closed. The trials are held on a 15-mile circuit, starting and finishing in St Johns. The circuit travels towards Douglas, makes a left turn at Ballacraine and follows the road through to Kirkmichael, before heading south back to Peel, then east back to St Johns.

1907

Due to the success of the ACC Trials and the enthusiasm developing among Britain's top riders of the time — not least Matchless founders Harold and Charles Collier — the idea of making the Isle of Man races a permanent 'event' emerges. The organisers

were keen to keep the machines as close to standard customer machines as possible — 'tourers' — thus the TT name evolves.

May 28. The maiden TT event is split into two classes for Single and Twin-cylinder machines. The inaugural winners are Charlie Collier who averages over 38mph in winning the Single event aboard a Matchless, while Rem Fowler takes a Norton to victory in the Twin category.

1908-1910

Speeds and machine category change rapidly. By 1910 the TT is for 500cc Singles and 670cc Twins. Charlie Collier wins his second and final TT at over 50mph. It is some achievement, considering the roads are little more than dust bowls and the race lasts in excess of three hours. Indeed such is the concern over the rapid increase in speeds that the decision is made to transfer the 1911 races to the Mountain Circuit, part of which has been used by the RAC for its Gordon Bennet car race trials.

1911

The 'Mountain Circuit' takes its name from the Manx mountain lanes which climb in excess of 2,000 feet from sea level. The

track starts in Douglas and heads west towards Peel, but veers right at Ballacraine. Then following the road, as per the St John's circuit, the riders bypass the previous Kirkmichael turn off and head through to Ramsey before entering the treacherous mountain climb and heading back towards Douglas. The circuit is nearly 38 miles long!

The year also sees the first ever Junior (300cc singles/340cc twins) and Senior (500cc singles/585cc twins) classes. The first TT winner on the 'Mountain Circuit' is J Evans on a Humber twin. His average speed is a seemingly modest 41.45mph. Oscar Godfrey wins the Senior race, heading home an historic 1-2-3 for Indian V-twin machines. This remains the only TT win for a manufacturer from the United States.

1912

TT organisers drop single and twin restrictions. The Junior race is to be run to 350cc and the Senior to 500cc capacity.

1914

Crash helmets are made compulsory! The start/finish line moves to the top of Bray Hill (from Quarterbridge Road). Eric Williams (Junior) and Cyril Pullin

(Senior) are the last pre-Great War TT winners. Williams' victory is the first TT win for AJS.

1920

The first TT races to be held after the war are run on yet another (slightly) changed circuit. The start line moves to Glencrutchery Road, and the circuit now runs on through Cronk-ny-Mona to Signpost Corner, down to the Governor's Bridge and back along Glencrutchery Road. This is exactly as the course remains in 1997.

Eric Williams is unfortunate not to become a winner either side of the war. Despite setting a Junior lap record at over 51mph he retires with mechanical failure. Cyril Williams wins, despite having a 20-minute lead slashed to nine minutes on the final lap after hitting gearbox problems at Keppel Gate. Tommy De La Hay takes a Sunbeam to victory in the Senior race and becomes the first man to average over 50mph for a race on the 'new' Mountain Circuit.

1922

The introduction of the Lightweight event for 250cc machines now makes the TT a three-race event. Geoff Davison is the inaugural winner.

1909
Riders corner the 'wrong way round' at Ballacraine during the 1909 TT, approaching Peel from St John's rather than Douglas. (Mick Woollett Archive)

1922
Lightweight 250 TT: Winner Geoff Davison (Levis) rounds Ramsey Hairpin. He went on to found the TT Special. (Mick Woollett Archive)

1935
Stanley Woods is congratulated after his famous Senior TT win of 1935. Riding a Moto Guzzi V-twin, he beat Jimmy Guthrie by four seconds with a record-breaking last lap. (Mick Woollett Archive)

Concerns rise again regarding speeds, and a rift emerges between the ACU and the Manx Government which nearly results in the TT being moved to the British mainland. Common sense prevails.

1923

A sidecar race is added to the programme. Freddie Dixon takes his famous 'banking' Douglas to victory. A young Southern Irishman by the name of Stanley Woods confirms the promise shown the previous year by taking a Cotton to victory in the Junior race.

1924

The first-ever 60mph lap had nearly been achieved in 1923 by Jimmy Simpson. Not only is the '60' mark achieved in '24, it is completely shattered as Simpson laps at 64.54mph in the Junior event. However, his AJS eventually expires. A host of retirements lets in a surprised Ken Twemlow for victory aboard a New Imperial.

1925

New records. Eddie Twemlow becomes the first to win the same race in successive years taking a New Imperial to victory in the Lightweight 250cc. Previously unlucky, Wal Handley finally breaks his TT 'duck' in becoming the first to win two TT races in a week as he cruises through the Junior and Ultra Lightweight events.

1926

Methanol fuel is banned and competitors must use ordinary petrol.

First TT visits for Italian marques Moto Guzzi, Bianchi, and Garelli. Pietro Ghersi (Guzzi) 'wins' the Lightweight race, only to be disqualified for an administrative error on the type of spark plug used!

Jimmy Simpson breaks the 70mph mark in the Senior event aboard his AJS, yet victory again eludes him. Stanley Woods claims the win on a Norton.

Alec Bennett becomes first man to win three TT races as he takes the Junior on his Velocette.

1928

Following the death of Archie Birkin the previous year after colliding with a fish lorry during morning training, the organisers close the roads for practice sessions as well as for the race.

Alec Bennett wins a record-setting fifth TT by taking a Velocette to victory in the Junior event.

1930

Soon to be legendary, Scot Jimmy Guthrie wins his maiden TT aboard an AJS in the Lightweight race.

1931

Norton-mounted Percy 'Tim' Hunt becomes the first man to win the Junior and Senior double.

Jimmy Simpson is at it again. He breaks the 80mph barrier in the Senior race lapping at 80.82mph. But he hasn't won a race.

1932-33

Stanley Woods emulates 'Tim' Hunt by winning the Junior-Senior double in both years. This takes him to a record breaking six TT wins.

1934

Jimmy Simpson finally wins a TT — the Lightweight!

1935

Stanley Woods takes his seventh and eighth TT wins in the Lightweight and Senior races — aboard Moto Guzzis, thus providing the first TT wins for a 'European' marque.

1937

Jimmy Guthrie wins his sixth and final TT win in the Junior event. Tragically Guthrie dies at the Sachsenring just six weeks after the TT.

Onobono Tenni becomes the first Italian to officially win a TT, taking a Moto Guzzi to victory in the Lightweight race. Freddie Frith (Norton) becomes the first man to lap the circuit over 90mph on his way to winning an historic Senior race from Stanley Woods.

1938

Ewald Kluge gives Germany its first rider/manufacturer TT win taking a DKW to victory in the Lightweight event. Kluge's lap record of 80.35mph means that all three classes are now lapping in excess of 80mph. Harold Daniell ups the lap record to 91mph on a Norton in the Senior, in one of the TT's finest ever races. Bespectacled Daniell beats off the Velocette challenge of Stanley Woods and young team-mate Freddie Frith.

1939

Again the Germans grab the headlines. With political tensions growing in Europe, Georg Maier takes a supercharged BMW to Senior victory. Norton, by now, is already committed to military contracts and 'only' sends its 1938 models to the event.

Stanley Woods wins his tenth and last TT aboard a Velocette in the Junior event.

1947

Racing resumes with the FIM banning supercharged machines. Harold Daniell, who had actually been turned down as a despatch rider during the war, wins the Senior event. Freddie Frith takes the Junior.

TT Chronicle 1907-1997

1949

1961

1949

Junior TT . J Kentish (6) and Les Martin paddle away down the Glencrutchery Road. Howard Daniell (Norton — 9) and Les Graham (AJS — 10) prepare to move to the start line. The race is won by Freddie Firth on a Velocette. (Mick Woollett Archive)

1961

Post Senior after Mike Hailwood (left) has taken a Norton to victory. Celebrating with him are (left to right), Bill Lacey, Stan Hailwood and Bob McIntyre. (Nick Nicholls)

1958

MV wins all four solo classes. The victorious riders are Ubbiali (125cc), Provini (Lightweight), and Surtees (Junior and Senior).

A youngster named Mike Hailwood makes his TT debut. Sammy Miller throws away a certain TT win by falling from his Mondial at Governor's on the last lap of the Lightweight race.

1959

John Surtees extends the out-right lap record at the end of the decade to 101.18mph in notching his third Senior TT victory.

This is the final year of the Clypse Course. From 1960 all races will be run on the Mountain Circuit.

Honda makes its TT debut in the 125cc event without much success.

Mike Hailwood makes more of an impression, gaining his first podium placing in the same race.

1960

In his final TT, John Surtees wins the Senior TT again, his sixth outright TT victory, and the lap record is up to 104.08mph.

Derek Minter becomes first man to take a single-cylinder machine round the mountain circuit at over 100mph.

1961

The previously unimpressive Honda machines make everyone stand up and take notice. With the young Mike Hailwood on board, the Japanese machines

1949

The TT is now part of the newly-formed FIM World Championship. Frith and Daniell again win the Junior and Senior races for Velocette and Norton respectively. Mancliff Barrington wins the Lightweight for Moto Guzzi. Average speeds are still some way from matching pre-war standards.

1950

The arrival of a young Lancastrian rider in the Norton team sends shock waves through the TT establishment. Geoff Duke wins an historic Senior from more experienced team-mates Artie Bell and Johnny Lockett. Duke ups the outright lap record to 93.33mph for good measure.

1951

Geoff Duke completes a Junior-Senior double. He takes 350cc machines over 90mph for the first time, and the 500cc lap record is up to 95.22mph.

1952

Reg Armstrong wins the Senior race on a Norton, having his chain break as he crosses the line. Duke had earlier retired with clutch failure while leading.

Cecil Sandford gives MV Agusta its first TT victory by winning the 125cc Ultra Lightweight.

1953

Rhodesian Ray Amm gives Norton another Junior-Senior double. Amm also raises the lap record stakes to 97.41mph. The Senior race is marred by tragedy, however, as fan favourite Les Graham is killed following an accident at the bottom of Bray Hill at the start of the second lap. Ironically Graham had won his first TT that morning, taking an MV to victory in the 125cc race.

1954

The advent of a new circuit for the 125cc and returning Sidecar class. The Clypse Course is near-ly 11 miles long, and uses part of the Mountain Circuit in reverse, from Cronk-ny-Mona through to Creg-ny-Baa. The course then winds down over the top of Onchan and proceeds through Onchan village, up to Signpost and then follows the main circuit back to start/finish. The inaugur-al Clypse winners are Rupert Hollaus of Austria in the 125cc event, while Eric Oliver takes the sidecar race.

Hollaus' NSU team mate Werner Haas wins the 250cc race on the Mountain Circuit and laps a 250cc machine at over 90mph for the first time.

Ray Amm, retains his Senior crown in controversial manner as the race is stopped after four of the six laps due to appalling weather conditions.

1955

The100mph barrier comes so close — it's actually announced over the PA that Geoff Duke, in winning his first TT for Gilera, has broken the magic 'ton up' lap on the third tour. Unfortunately for Duke and TT fans in general, Geoff's official lap was 'only' 99.97mph.

BMW powers Walter Schneider to the first of what will be many sidecar TT wins.

This is the first year a British motorcycle hasn't won a TT race.

1956

John Surtees wins his first TT — the Senior for MV. Duke (and the entire Gilera team) is missing as he is under FIM suspension for backing pay scale rows the previ-ous year.

1957

Gilera finally breaks the 100mph barrier, but it's not Geoff Duke who does it — he is sidelined by injury. Scot, Bob McIntyre wins an epic eight-lap Senior and sets a lap record of 101.12mph on the second tour. He laps at over 100mph three more times during the race. McIntyre also wins the Junior race.

1951

1962

1959

1951
Geoff Duke at Creg-ny-Baa during his Senior TT winning ride aboard the Norton. He set a new lap record in this race (95.22mph), and took the Junior lap record to over 90mph for the first time. (Mick Woollett Archive)

1959
John Surtees leaps the MV Agusta over Ballaugh Bridge during the Senior. He won the race and extended the lap record to 101.18mph. (Nick Nicholls)

1963
Ernst Degner, pictured at Governor's Bridge, scored Suzuki's maiden TT win on this 50cc machine. (Nick Nicholls)

1962
Another Suzuki milestone. Another 50cc race win, but this time it's the first-ever win for a Japanese rider — Mitsuo Itoh. (Nick Nicholls)

are victorious in the 125cc and Lightweight races.

Yamaha and Suzuki add more Oriental flavour. Fumio Ito brings the former marque home in an impressive sixth place in the 250cc race, while Hugh Anderson finishes tenth in the same race aboard a Suzuki.

Hailwood sensationally becomes the first man to win three TTs in one week, when he takes a single-cylinder Norton to victory in the Senior.

Phil Read wins his first TT (less than a year after winning the MGP) — the Junior on a Norton. It's the first Junior-Senior wins for British machinery since 1954.

1962

Swiss-Italian Luigi Taveri becomes the first rider to take a 125cc machine round the Mountain Circuit at over 90mph aboard a Honda. Derek Minter also on a Honda takes the 250cc race.

Mike Hailwood has now switched to MV and he and team-mate Gary Hocking are more or less unstoppable in the Junior race. Hailwood takes the 350cc lap record over the ton barrier for the first time. Hocking wins the Senior, and sets a new outright lap record of 105.75mph.

Ernst Degner scores a famous victory for Suzuki in the maiden 50cc TT race.

Beryl Swain becomes the first woman to compete in a solo TT race. She finishes 22nd in the 50cc race.

1963

Honda has now upped the ante into the Junior category. Rhodesian Jim Redman scores his first two TT wins adding a 250cc victory to the Junior win scored earlier in the week.

The 500cc lap record has gone up again. This time it's Mike Hailwood taking an MV round at 106.41mph.

Mitsuo Itoh becomes first Japanese TT winner by taking the 50cc laurels for Suzuki.

1965

Yamaha challenges Honda hard in the Lightweight class and an epic race between Phil Read and Jim Redman falls in the Rhodesian's favour. Read retires while leading. Redman isn't hanging around and establishes the first 100mph lap for a 250cc machine in winning his sixth and final TT.

Read gains some revenge by winning the 125cc race — Yamaha's first TT win.

Max Deubel takes the sidecar

1963

boys over the 90mph barrier.

MV introduces a new Italian starlet, Giacomo Agostini. 'Ago' finishes third in the Junior race.

TT Chronicle 1907-1997

1967

1968

1966

A seamans' strike in June, postpones the TT. The TT and the Manx Grand Prix are run back-to-back — four weeks of non-stop bike action!

Agostini returns with style, and wins the Junior race for MV.

Mike Hailwood has now returned to Honda. While the British rider may be struggling in the World Championships, he is still the TT rider to beat and takes TT wins eight and nine with victory in the 250cc and Senior races. The Senior lap record goes up to 107.07mph.

1967

The TT Diamond Jubilee. Mike Hailwood repeats his feat of 1961 by winning another three races in a week to eclipse Stanley Woods' record of ten TT wins. Mike's first win comes in the Junior event, taking the Honda to a new lap record on a 350cc machine! Victory number two is in the 250cc event. It is the 500cc win, however, that will go down in history as perhaps one of the greatest motorcycle races ever held, with Ago making it hard work for Hailwood in the Senior. Ago's chain breaks on the Mountain on the fifth lap. He returns to the pits in tears, on this his 25th birthday, as the TT Maestro completes his 12th TT win. The lap record is raised to 108.77mph.

The Production TT is run for the first time. John Hartle is a popular winner in the 750cc class aboard a Triumph.

Siegfried Schauzu scores a maiden TT sidecar victory.

1968

Honda and Suzuki pulled out of racing at the end of the previous season, leaving MV to conquer the 350cc and 500cc categories, and Yamaha to dominate the lightweight divisions. While Agostini rules an easy roost in his two classes, some inbred rivalry within the Yamaha camp brings two fabulous races in the 125cc and 250cc divisions.

Phil Read and Bill Ivy make no secret of their dislike of each other. Yamaha has stated that Read should win the 125cc race and Ivy the 250cc. Ivy duly takes the 250cc honours, raising the lap record to 105.51mph in the process, but Read runs him close before retiring. In the 125cc race, however, Ivy decides to show Read and Yamaha exactly how good he is. The little British rider storms off into the lead and subsequently sets a new lap record of 100.32mph — an outstanding achievement for a 125cc machine. Ivy, having made his mark, slows on the final lap to let Read win, as he promised to do.

1969

A nondescript year with Yamaha also having withdrawn official support, although Dave Simmonds gives the fourth Japanese manufacturer, Kawasaki, its first TT win by taking 125cc honours.

1970

Danger raises its ugly head again as six riders are killed during practice and race weeks. They include promising Irishman

Brian Steenson and Spanish 250cc stalwart Santiago Herrero.

Agostini completes his third Junior-Senior double in succession.

1971

Sensation as Agostini doesn't win a race. His MV fails on the first lap of the Junior in Ramsey, and Tony Jefferies sweeps to his second win of the week, adding to his victory in the inaugural F750cc race.

1972

World Championship status for the event is already threatened and the situation is compounded by the death of 125cc world championship leader Gilberto Parlotti, who crashes in thick mist while leading the 125cc race. Agostini and Phil Read are damning in their criticism of the place, although it doesn't stop Ago completing a fourth Junior-Senior double. These will be his last TT wins, giving him ten overall.

1973

The GP 'stars' stay away and the TT takes on a very British flavour, although Australian Jack Findlay takes a fine Senior victory aboard his Suzuki. Peter Williams leads Mick Grant home in a JPS Norton 1-2 in the F750 race.

1967
Hailwood gets under way at the start of the 1967 Senior for what is about to become one of the great TT races of all time. After battling with Agostini, who eventually retires with a broken chain, Hailwood makes it 12 TT victories and sets a new lap record in the process. (Mick Woollett Archive)
1968
Ago rules the roost in the Senior and Junior. This is the Senior aboard the MV three at Braddan Bridge. (Nick Nicholls)
1973
Peter Williams at Ramsey on the John Player Norton during the F750 race. He led Mick Grant home on a JPN 1-2. (Nick Nicholls)

1975

Mike Hailwood's eight-year-old outright lap record is shattered by Mick Grant aboard a 750cc Kawasaki in the Classic TT, which formally takes over from the Senior as the Blue Ribband of the TT. Grant's record lap is recorded at 109.82mph. However, the 'Kwaka' expires and John Williams takes a popular victory, broken collar-bone and all, aboard a 350cc Yamaha!

1976

The final year of 'Grand Prix' status. Takazumi Katayama makes his TT debut, thus provid-

1976
Tom Herron set a new lap record in the 250 race on his way to victory ahead of Takazumi Katayama. Both riders were on Yamahas. This was the final year the TT boasted Grand Prix status. (Nick Nicholls)

1979
Hailwood returns, Hailwood wins. Mike 'the Bike' had works Suzukis in 1979 and won the Senior. He also finished second in the Classic TT. (Nick Nicholls)

1992
Last TT win for a British bike? After a cracking scrap with Yamaha-mounted Carl Fogarty, Steve Hislop won the Senior on the ABUS Norton — Norton's first TT win in 20 years. (Terry Howe)

ing three of the top four 250cc riders in the world at the event. It is a fine race, but Ulsterman Tom Herron's superior course knowledge prevails and he heads Katayama home. Chas Mortimer is third.

John Williams ups the outright lap record aboard a works 500cc Suzuki in the Senior. Unfortunately, the bike starts to suffer from fuel starvation problems on the run down the Mountain on the final lap and victory escapes him.

Tom Herron on a 350 Yamaha is declared winner. Williams receives some recompense by taking a Classic TT win.

A young Irishman called Dunlop makes his TT debut.

Siggi Schauzu establishes a record ninth sidecar TT victory.

1977

With FIM blessing, the ACU introduces its own 'World Championship' for Formula One, Two, and Three machines. Previous TT critic Phil Read returns and promptly becomes the first F1 winner aboard a works Honda.

Read also takes a private Suzuki to victory in the Senior event.

Dick Greasley goes down in the history books as the first man to

break the 100mph barrier on a sidecar.

Joey Dunlop scores a maiden TT win in the Jubilee TT — run to National status.

1978

Mike Hailwood makes a sensational return to the TT, 11 years after his last ride on the Island. He is armed with a works Ducati for the F1 race and wins at a canter. He ups the F1 lap record to 110.62mph.

Mike has cruel luck in the remaining races for which he is aboard the works Yamahas.

Tragedy strikes in the Senior race. World 500cc Championship leader Pat Hennen crashes while chasing leader Tom Herron on the last lap. He suffers severe head injuries. The American had raised the outright lap record to 113.83mph.

Hennen's record lasts just four days as Mick Grant raises the lap speed to 114.33mph on his way to an easy Classic race win.

TT veteran Mac Hobson and passenger Kenny Birch are killed instantly in an horrific accident on Bray Hill.

Swiss driver Ernst Traschel also succumbs to fatal injuries in a separate accident on Bray Hill. Altogether five competitors are killed at TT78.

1979

Hailwood returns for what he promises will be his last TT, aboard a factory 500cc Suzuki. He wins again in the Senior event, but only after Scot Alex George retires his Cagiva while battling for the lead. George had been a surprising F1 winner on a factory Honda.

Alex and Mike line up to do battle in the Classic TT — it turns out to be just that — a Classic, with barely seconds between them throughout the six laps. A last spurt over the Mountain puts George ahead to score an historic win.

Charlie Williams breaks Bill Ivy's 11-year 250cc lap record.

1980

Despite being on the verge of retiring from racing, Joey Dunlop battles the works Suzuki of Mick Grant, and a broken fuel tank strap, for Classic TT honours. Joey is aboard a private TZ750cc Yamaha yet he shatters the lap record at 115.22mph. Joey's retirement plans go on the backburner.

Charlie Williams wins his last two TT races on the same day, taking Mitsui Yamahas to victory in the F2 and 250cc races.

Jock Taylor, a young Scottish

sidecar driver, steals TT fans hearts with a fabulous win in the second sidecar race.

1981

Joey Dunlop returns to the TT as a factory Honda rider. However, bad luck and controversy stalk Joey and Honda. In the F1 race Dunlop loses valuable time at his pit stop and seemingly hands victory to young teammate Ron Haslam. New Zealander Graeme Crosby is awarded his actual start time, as opposed to his intended start time, after missing the start of the race. Crosby is awarded victory on corrected time — much to Honda's chagrin.

Honda is still bitter a week later and its bikes and riders are turned out in black as a protest. Suzuki again has the last laugh though.

Dunlop raises the lap record to 115.40mp but runs out of fuel, and Crosby cruises to victory again.

1982

Ron Haslam wins his first (and only) TT aboard a works Honda in the F1 race.

Jock Taylor wins his fourth sidecar TT in three years and claims a lap record of 108.29mph.

TT Chronicle 1907-1997

1983

Joey Dunlop wins his first F1 TT and establishes another new course record of 115.73mph.

Dunlop's record lasts but a week, as fellow Irishman Norman Brown establishes an incredible lap of 116.19mph aboard a private 500cc Suzuki in the Senior Classic race. Brown runs out of petrol and Rob McElnea wins on a works-assisted Suzuki.

Con Law riding an EMC becomes the first man to lap the TT circuit at over 110mph on a 250cc machine. He wins into the bargain.

Mick Boddice wins his first sidecar TT after 16 years of trying.

1984

The lap record is broken again. This time it's Joey's turn. Having already won the F1 race, Joey again runs out of petrol, handing victory to Rob McElnea in the Senior TT but not before he sets a new 118.47mph yardstick on the way.

Production racing returns to the TT.

1985

Joey Dunlop becomes only the second man to win three TT races in a week. He takes F1, 250cc and Senior honours.

1986

Production racing takes the headlines. Trevor Nation laps at 113.26 mph in winning the 1100cc class. Mat Oxley takes a 250cc proddie bike round at over 100mph.

1987

Joey Dunlop wins F1 and Senior races to move onto ten TT wins.

Steve Hislop of Hawick takes a maiden TT win in the F2 event.

1988

Dunlop completes another TT hat trick. He also breaks the lap record again in the F1 race. It now stands at 118.54mph. However, although Dunlop wins the 250cc race and ultimately the Senior, it is fellow countryman, Steve Cull, who takes a slice of the headlines, establishing a new course record of 119.08mph as he battles with Dunlop, only for his RS500 Honda to catch fire at Cregny-Baa on the final lap.

Geoff Johnson sets an incredible lap speed of 116.55mph on a production machine.

1989

Tragedy strikes again as TT stalwarts Phil Mellor and Steve Henshaw are killed in separate accidents during the 1300cc Production race.

Steve Hislop matches Hailwood and Dunlop to score three TT wins in a week. He also sets a new lap record of 121.84mph in winning the F1 event. Joey is out through injury.

Mick Boddice now wins TT races with alarming regularity. He scores his seventh overall win and breaks Jock Taylor's lap record.

1990

Steve Hislop beats his own circuit lap record but is already well down the field in the F1 race after experiencing brake problems on the opening lap. He sets a magnificent lap speed of 122.63mph on the final tour — but finishes ninth. Carl Fogarty takes his first F1 win.

Sidecar races now run to F2 regulations. Dave Saville wins both races.

1991

Steve Hislop completes his second TT hat trick. As well as F1 and Senior victories, the Scot also wins the Supersport 600 race. The outright lap record is increased to 123.48mph — by Hislop.

Mick Boddice equals Siggi Schauzu's tally of nine TT wins by taking both sidecar races.

1992

Hislop is riding an ABUS-backed, works 588cc rotary-engined Norton for the first time. Arch rival Carl Fogarty also sets up a last-minute deal to ride an unfamiliar machine — a YZR750 Yamaha. Fogarty establishes an early lead in the F1 race, which quickly grows to a 40-second plus advantage by lap five, only for the gearbox to break. With Hislop's Norton suffering from over-heating problems, Phil McCallen picks up the pieces to give Honda another F1 win.

Joey Dunlop wins his first TT race for four years and equals Mike Hailwood on 14 victories.

The Hislop and Fogarty rivalry is renewed in the Senior race. Both break the lap record, firstly Hislop, but this is broken almost immediately by Fogarty — a staggering 123.61mph. But it's Hislop who wins by 4.4 seconds, giving Norton its first TT victory for nearly 20 years.

1993

Joey breaks Hailwood's record in establishing his 15th TT win by taking another 125cc victory.

1994

After a year's sabbatical, Hislop returns but is virtually unopposed in the F1 and Senior races aboard his RVF750 Honda. Joey Dunlop keeps racking up the wins taking victories number 16 and 17 in the 125cc and 250cc events.

1995

It's victory number 18 and 19 for Dunlop. He wins the 125cc and Senior races, silencing the critics who now say he can't ride the bigger-capacity machines. Hislop does not enter.

1996

Phillip McCallen sets a new record as he becomes the first man to win four TT races in one week. The Irishman wins the F1, Junior, newly-reinstated Production and Senior races.

Joey also keeps winning. He takes victory again in the 125cc and 250cc events and now has 21 overall victories. Dave Molyneux wins both sidecar races and becomes the first sidecar driver to lap at over 110mph.

Words: *Steve Burns*

1994

Yer Maestro! Another two wins take Joey Dunlop to 17 TT victories. This is on the 125 at Ramsey. (Terry Howe)

1996

Good golly, it's Moly! Dave Molyneux, with passenger Pete Hill, became the first sidecar duo to lap at over 110mph during their blistering double victory. (Terry Howe)

1996

Victory in sight as Bob McIntyre (Gilera, number 78) catches John Surtees (MV Agusta, number 64) as they accelerate out of Governor's Bridge dip during the memorable 1957 Senior TT. McIntyre took the outright course record beyond 100mph for the first time. Surtees, the 1956 Senior TT winner, finished second on this occasion. (Mick Woollett Archive)

Bob Mac's

Was it really 40 years ago that Bob McIntyre clocked the first ever 'ton' lap on the Isle of Man? That certainly makes me feel old because I can remember the day, Friday June 7, 1957, as though it was yesterday. It dawned bright and chilly with a brisk wind blowing patchy white clouds across the Manx skyline and my task as the junior reporter on Cyril Quantrill's then new 'Motor Cycle News', was to ferry our star photographer Tom Badger to various vantage points around the course.

Our transport was Cyril's 500cc BSA Gold Star and Watsonian sidecar; a marvellous combination which I really enjoyed riding and which in those days was more than a match for the majority of cars. Tom's favourite spot was Kate's Cottage. There he would lie in the road with his massive plate camera

and capture those classic shots of riders hurtling by the Cottage at speeds over 100mph.

My job, as well as transporting him, was to shout when a star rider was approaching. With a maximum of only 36 glass plates to expose he could not afford to waste any on also-rans. So that Friday morning we drove up to Creg-ny-Baa, parked the outfit so that it would not get blocked in and walked the half-mile up the road to Kate's.

Once there we chatted to the marshals. Naturally enough the talk centred on whether this was to be the big day — would the 100mph lap be

achieved at last? Of course TT enthusiasts had been talking of the 'ton' lap since the 1930s. Jimmie Simpson (Norton) had clocked the first 80mph lap for the 37.73 mile circuit as early as 1931 with a lap in 28m1.0s, 80.82mph.

The great Irishman Stanley Woods pushed the figure over the 85mph mark in 1935 with an epic last lap on the V-twin Moto Guzzi during which he cut no less than 1m 12s off his own record (set on a Norton in 1933) to beat his Norton-mounted rival Jimmy Guthrie by just 4s, Woods' time was 26m 10s, 86.53mph.

Such was the pace of progress, and

h100mph 100mp

Ton-up Lap

What were you doing on June 7, 1957? Mick Woollett was at Kate's Cottage to witness Bob McIntyre become the first man

record finally went. Duke, who had won the previous year's Senior Manx Grand Prix on a 'garden gate' Norton with a record lap at 25m 53s, 87.48mph, lapped at 90.27mph during practise — the first ever 90mph circuit since pre-war days, but still short of Daniell's 91mph.

In the actual race Duke led all the way, shattering both race and lap records. In fact, his average speed for the seven-lap 264.11 mile race was 92.37mph, faster than Daniell's old lap record and some 3mph better than Georg Meier's BMW 1939 race record. Duke's new lap record was 24m 16s, 93.33mph — the magic 'ton' was obviously just a matter of time.

In 1951 Duke won again for Norton, slicing no less than 29s off his record time to lap in 23m 47s, 95.22mph. That record stood until 1953. By that time Duke had switched to Gilera but he could not match the pace of the incredible Ray Amm who had taken over as Norton's number one. Their battle ended when Duke crashed at Quarter Bridge leaving Amm to win at a record 93.85 mph and with a record lap at 23m 15s, 97.41mph — 32s better than the old record and only 37s short of the

This is the 500cc four-cylinder Gilera, McIntyre rode to win the 1957 Senior TT and clock the first ton lap of the TT circuit. (Mick Woollett Archive)

road improvements, that the 90mph barrier went just two years later. This time the man in the saddle was Freddie Frith who circulated on his Norton in 25m 5s, 90.27mph to beat Woods (now Velocette mounted) by just 15s. Teammate Harold Daniell pushed the record up to exactly 91mph (24m 52.6s) when he won the Senior in 1938 (again Woods on his factory Velocette was second this time 15.2s astern) and there the record stuck for 12 years.

Why so long? The facts are that after the war the FIM, the sport's governing body, banned both high octane fuel (pre-war alcohol was banned but riders

were allowed to use a 50-50 mixture of petrol and benzol which had an octane rating close to 100) and superchargers. With competitors limited to 'pool' petrol with, in the early post-war years, an octane rating of little over 70 (the lowest you can get today is around 90!) speeds were cut dramatically.

It was only in 1950 when the advent of the 'feathered' Norton coincided with improved fuel, coupled with the brilliance of TT newcomer Geoff Duke — that Daniell's

Bob Mac's ton-up lap

100mph lap.

The next year Amm won again for Norton in a race cut short by appalling weather which scuppered any chance of record speeds — in fact the best round, by the Rhodesian, was at just 89.82mph! But for close on an hour in 1955 we thought the 'ton' target had been achieved, for Duke set a scorching pace on his works Gilera and on his third lap he got round in 22m 39s — a time that equalled 100mph on some lap charts.

However, when this was checked, it was found that the speed was actually 99.97mph. Duke's disappointment was more than compensated for by his first

Bob McIntyre is hugged by his mother after his record-breaking win on the works four-cylinder Gilera. Left, holding a programme, is Feruccio Gilera, team manager and son of founder Giuseppe. (Mick Woollett)

Right: McIntyre waves as he is congratulated by his mother after his sensational eight-lap 1957 Senior TT victory on the Gilera — and the first 100mph lap. (Mick Woollett)

Gilera Senior TT success — and among the first to congratulate him was the firm's founder Commendatore Giuseppe Gilera.

Banned from racing for the first half of the 1956 because of his support for the private riders at the previous year's Dutch TT — probably the most infamous act of the FIM in the history of motorcycle sport — Duke had no chance to attack the 100mph lap in 1956 and in far from ideal conditions not even race winner John Surtees (MV Augusta) could get anywhere near the 'ton'.

It seemed that fate was conspiring against Duke, for in 1957 he crashed early in the season at Imola and was not fit to race in the TT. This meant that Bob McIntyre was promoted to number one for the Italian team with Australian Bob Brown signed as second-string. In the Junior, McIntyre — at his brilliant best on the TT circuit — signalled his intentions by shattering Amm's three-year-old Norton record of 94.61mph with a lap at 97.42mph.

If the flying Scot could do that on a 350 what would he do on the 500? That was the topic of conversation all around the course, not least at Kate's Cottage where Tom Badger and I waited for the action. That year was the Golden Jubilee of the TT and the organisers had decided to lengthen the race from the usual seven to eight laps — no less than 301.84 gruelling miles, four times longer than today's 500cc championship 'sprints'.

Unlike Duke, who preferred the abbreviated handlebar fairing, McIntyre opted for the full 'dustbin' style of streamlining that was outlawed at the end of the season. His Gilera developed around 70bhp at 10,500rpm to give a top speed of about 145mph. This gave the Scot a definite edge over Surtees on the heavier and slightly less powerful MV Augusta. In those days, the riders were not 'seeded' according to ability and Surtees, the only rider in with a real chance of challenging McIntyre, started at number 64 some two minutes ahead of the Gilera that carried number 78. But by the time they reached us at Kate's, it was obvious that the Scot had cut the Londoner's time margin and was well ahead in the race. Fortunately the white and scarlet 'dustbin' made the Gilera easy to spot and I can remember shouting to Tom, who panned frantically as McIntyre swept by — plunging down the hill to Creg-ny-Baa with the crowd waving and urging him on. Soon the news filtered through to us via portable radios in the crowd. McIntyre had broken Duke's two-year-old lap record from a standing start. He had circulated in 22m 38.4s — a speed of 99.99mph! He'd missed the ton by a fifth of a second — the smallest margin the time keepers worked to.

If he could keep it up, the first ever 100mph lap was sure to be achieved on his first flying lap. And so it proved to be, McIntyre lapped at 22m 24.4s and went right through the 'ton' barrier, for the speed worked out to 101.03mph. By that time he was well ahead and in response to signals (he had no less than four signalling stations around the course that day including Geoff Duke

and his former Gilera team-mate Reg Armstrong at Sulby) he slowed slightly.

On his third lap he averaged 100.54 mph then speeded to up the lap record to 22m 23.2s, 101.12mph, despite slowing down to stop and refuel at the end of the lap, the halfway mark. Bob had no idea that he had bettered the 'ton' and his mechanic, the veteran Gilera spannerman Giovanni Fumagalli, did not tell him. In any case he was not particularly worried. His aim was to win the race.

Incredibly his fifth and sixth lap times were within 5s of one another. Then he slowed and, with the race in the bag, cut his pace by half a minute a lap and, in his own words, 'toured' in to win — mindful that the race was twice the distance of most grand prix events of the time. Despite this, his average of 98.99mph easily beat Duke's old race record.

However, Tom and I never did see the finish. Halfway through the race we had to run down to the Creg, kick-start the Gold Star into life and do our bit of racing to get to Ronaldsway Airport in the south of the island in time to get Tom's precious photographic plates on the plane to London. Two things stand out in my memory about the trip. First I went into the right-hander over the railway bridge just beyond the Fairy Bridge too fast and just managed to scramble round the rear wheel in the air, with poor Tom cursing and swearing as he clung to the precious plates — and second, a moment of elation as I caught up with 'Motor Cycling' photographer 'Flasher' Long in his Morris Minor, and out-braked him into the left-hander at Ballasalla. Great days.

Words: *Mick Woollett*

Stanley Woods

Stanley Woods was a TT regular in the 1920s. He won the 1923 Junior TT at 55.73mph on this 350cc Blackburne-engined Cotton. (Mick Woollett Archive)

Opposite: Woods won five TTs on Nortons from 1926 to 1933 including Junior/Senior doubles in 1932 and 1933. This picture was taken in 1931 — but at the Belgian GP and not on the Island. (Mick Woollett Archive)

Riding works Nortons he won 20 GP races, including four TTs, then Stanley Woods shocked the industry by pursuing more lucrative deals to ride faster, foreign machinery.

Shrewd & DETERMINED

Statistics count of course — but what is it that makes a true superstar, a rider who stands head and shoulders above his contemporaries? A rider who, without question, captures the imagination, the loyalty and the downright adoration of the masses who follow motorcycle sport?

Four such men spring to mind. All carried an almost tangible air of daring and style, and a stoic dignity in the face of adversity. Walter Handley, Geoff Duke, even Mike Hailwood — none of them exactly travelled through a bed of roses in their rise to the top. Stanley Woods didn't either, and his undeniable stardom was very much a matter of his will and dogged determination, the outcome of a shrewd and reasoned strategy that ran through his later career.

Stanley was born in Dublin in 1903 and even as a boy was a motorcycle enthusiast. His first taste of competition was in sprints and handicap races with his father's Harley Davidson — with and without its sidecar.

Fellow Dublin club member, pre-war Rudge rider Tommy Green, taught Stanley all he knew ("My mentor" Stanley called him) and aroused his enthusiasm for the TT in the Isle of Man. With his friend C W 'Paddy' Johnston and the faithful Harley, Stanley visited the TT in 1921 — and was hooked for ever more!

By some monumental bluffing, he wangled his entry in the 1922 Junior on one of the new ohv Cotton Blackburnes. Despite Willoughby

> *"I didn't really regard myself as a racing motorcyclist... it wasn't until Norton approached me late in 1925 that I took the idea seriously."*

Cotton's dismay, ("My God! They've sent me a bloody schoolboy!") Stanley rode an heroic, if troubled, race. Despite two falls, a nasty fire in the pits, loss of brakes and a loose exhaust pipe, he finished fifth — and brought more publicity to Cotton than if he had won! And that he did again — with far less drama — in the 1923 Senior, once more on a Cotton Blackburne. Overnight he was famous, but for a few years his career languished. Why?. "Well I didn't really regard myself as a racing motorcyclist", he confessed. "I'd won a lot of money in 1923 and had visions of making a success in business. I started up making and selling 'TT Toffees' and it wasn't until Norton approached me late in 1925 that I took the idea seriously."

Racing for Norton entailed selling trips throughout the north of England, operating from a sidecar outfit. Not much fun, according to Stanley, but it did lead to a Senior TT win in 1926, on the last of the pushrod ohv Nortons! The 1927 Senior looked like a repeat performance on the new ohc CSI Norton, but alas, four minutes in the lead and having lapped at 70.90mph, his clutch failed, allowing Alec Bennett, his teammate to win. Woods blamed the Norton pit for having failed to tell him to ease the pace. Whether or not this was just, it led to his devising his own signalling system on the island.

In 1927, Stanley also won in Holland, Belgium and Switzerland, but thereafter Norton was very much under a cloud and did not recover until the arrival of the new Joe Craig engine of 1931. Over the next three seasons Woods and Norton scored no less than 20 Grand Prix wins including two 'double' Junior and Senior TTs. Stanley was indeed the outstanding rider of the day — and of the great Norton team.

Yet to universal astonishment he abruptly left Norton at the end of 1933. Why? "Purely because of money," Stanley admitted.

"Norton's way of sharing out prize money was no incentive to me. I had lost a lot in my business ventures, and at 30, I had a limited earning life.

"I was approached by Husqvarna and Moto Guzzi and I was in position to demand lucrative contracts — I never regretted the decision."

The Husqvarna V-twins were fast —

Stanley Woods Shrewd and determined

Woods handed out of big shock to the single-cylinder brigade when he took the V-twin Moto Guzzi Bicilindrica to a win in the 1935 Senior TT. He beat Norton's Jimmy Guthrie by four seconds. (Mick Woollett Archive)

Aboard a works Norton in 1931, Woods finished fourth in the Senior TT. (Mick Woollett Archive)

faster than the Nortons — but they were temperamental and unreliable. Nor did the factory carry out promised modifications for the 1934 TT. During practise Stanley discovered that his frame was bent. It subsequently broke — and he himself had to mend and reinforce it. Endless 'carburation' troubles were diagnosed at a late stage (by the Amal rep) as due to lack of oil control rings. And again, it was Stanley (and the Wellworthy rep) who had to rectify the deficiency using a lathe at the Douglas tram depot. In a wet race, Stanley made fastest Senior lap before running out of petrol — eight miles from the chequered flag.

Things were very different with Moto Guzzi, who could not have been more co-operative, and Stanley's good relationship with the firm lasted until the end of his life.

In 1935 he won the Lightweight TT for them, and followed this by winning perhaps the most exciting Senior TT of all time on the 500cc even-firing Bicilindrica V-twin.

Lying second to Jimmy Guthrie's Norton at the start of the last lap, Stanley threw caution to the winds, revved the V-twin to bursting point and knocked no less than 1 minute 12 seconds from his own previous lap record for Norton (raising the speed by 4mph) to win by four vital seconds!

For 1936 Moto Guzzi did not contest the TT but Stanley, for a lucrative fee, rode a DKW in the Lightweight race. The relationship was not a happy one, and though Stanley made fastest lap,

> "Norton's way of sharing out prize money was no incentive to me... at 30, I had a limited earning life. I was approached by Husqvarna and Moto Guzzi and I was in position to demand lucrative contracts."

he retired as a direct consequence of DKW's refusal to fit a rev-counter!

By now he had been retained by Velocette, who had wanted his services for some time but had been inhibited from approaching him by works rider Walter Handley. With Walter having retired from motorcycle racing, Stanley was able to sort out Velocette's considerable problems and to materially assist with the development of its pioneering new spring frame. He was rewarded by a second place (and fastest lap at 86.98mph) in the Senior TT. Again in 1937 he rode a Velocette to second in the Senior, though he retired in the Lightweight (on a Moto Guzzi) whilst in the lead on the last lap. For 1938 Stanley and Velocette planned an

heroic programme of eight Grand Prix entries, but a serious crash in Belgium frustrated the whole programme.

However, before that, Stanley brought Velocette its first TT win for nine years in the Junior TT and yet another second place in the Senior.

Stanley's last racing season was in 1939, and the year brought another Junior TT win. He was also fourth in the Senior, but retired (after making fastest lap) in the waterlogged Lightweight race riding a supercharged Moto Guzzi. So ended Stanley Woods' 17-year riding career. In later years he managed Moto Guzzi's early post-war entries at the TT. Later still he appeared in the TT parades on several of the machines he had ridden pre-war, ably restored by his friend Ivan Rhodes. In 1956 he was invited by Moto Guzzi to Italy to try out its current racing motorcycles including the fabulous 500cc V8. Full of age and honours, Stanley Woods, winner of ten TTs died, aged 89 at the end of July 1993.

Words: *Brian Wooley*

T'RUDGING to TT success

Wal Handley's 1930 Senior TT-winning Ulster 500.

T hink of Rudge, and think of engines with four valves per cylinder — today a common enough two-wheeled design feature, but decidedly avant-garde back in 1923 when Rudge boss John Pugh introduced it to his model range. Rudge was never a large-volume manufacturer on the scale of BSA or Triumph.

Even in its best-selling years from 1926-29, Rudge's annual production was just 7,000 bikes, a scant 1% of the total British motorcycle market that peaked at 731,000 machines in 1929. But the company carved out a solid reputation for sound, reliable engineering, which incorporated advanced ideas that actually worked.

The 1920s were a time of great technical innovation in British motorcycle design — Norton and Velocette introduced overhead camshaft models, the positive stop gearchange was pioneered by Velocette's Harold Willis — but Rudge achieved success, both on the track and in the showroom, with two features which find continued expression today; coupled brakes — and the four-valve cylinder head.

Paired valves were nothing new on motorcycles even back then — the French marques Alcyon and Peugeot had multi-valve motors as far back as 1912, Indian introduced the concept to America on its board racers soon after (to be copied by Harley and others in turn on their racing machines). Meanwhile in Italy Moto Guzzi proved the idea's potential by winning the inaugural European Championship in 1924 with a four-valve overhead-cam 500, which started to explore the benefits of improved breathing delivered by paired valves.

In Britain, though, Triumph had pioneered the concept with its Ricardo-designed four-valver introduced in 1921 — but by 1928, it was out of production, leaving only Rudge to promote the concept on its road bikes. It sought to underline its benefits by success on the race track — especially in the Isle of Man TT.

Born out of a merger between two well-respected Midlands bicycle manufacturers, Rudge-Whitworth (as the company was properly called) consistently headed the British motorcycle industry's export league table in the Pioneer era — indeed, it was contracts from the Russian and Italian armies that kept the company afloat during the Great War.

Post-World War One, Rudge's John Pugh was a keen advocate of competition as a  means of promoting his products — and with Rudge's foreign sales, that meant Grand Prix racing all over Europe, as well as the Isle of Man TT, success in which was top of every manufacturer's wish-list.

While Rudge won the Senior TT in 1914 with its famous Multi (as in gearbox ratios, not cylinders — or valves!), it didn't enjoy much racing success thereafter — not until Graham Walker joined up from Sunbeam at the end of 1927 as rider/sales director, working alongside development chief George Hack, who also

Cathcart gets
down to the biz.
Handling of the
rigid-framed, gird-
er-forked
machine is excel-
lent, and steering
is light and pre-
dictable. But
then he didn't
have to ride the
TT course in
1930!

Wal Handley on the Rudge after winning the 1930 Senior TT. Standing with him, looking pleased as punch, is rider/sponsor Jim Whalley. Handley took over Whalley's entry but got factory equipment for the race against team boss, John Pugh's original judgement. The works riders sportingly banded together persuading Pugh to give Handley the team's best bike!

acted as team manager.

A prized win in the 1928 Senior TT, seemed on the cards when Walker led by no less than three minutes going into the last lap, only to be sidelined by big end failure with victory in his sights. Some compensation came, however, with success in the Dutch GP — and then, after a torrid battle with Dodson's Sunbeam, in that year's Ulster GP — the first time a road race had been won at an average speed of more than 80mph.

To commemorate that, Rudge's four-valve Sports model, closely derived from its works racer, was renamed the Ulster, a name that stayed in production for the next decade, and became synonymous with the marque.

In 1929, Rudge set several world speed records, took victory in the Brooklands 200-mile race at over 100mph, swept the ISDT Team Prize with an array of gold medals, and won the Dutch, German, Czech, South African, Spanish, Italian and Austrian GPs as well as the Ulster once again. But victory in the Senior TT remained unfinished business.

The Rudge team, the dominant force in world-class motorcycle racing, saw their greatest prize snatched from them

when Irishman Tyrell Smith, was set to win the Senior TT as he started his last lap — only to crash at the Highlander with victory once more in sight.

Tyrell remounted to finish third — but only after he'd been escorted into the pub there, revived with a large glass of alcoholic beverage, then on emerging from the bar been lifted onto his bike after it had been straightened and restarted by a group of spectators. All this theoretically contravened the rules. However, it was later discovered that he had broken four ribs in the crash, and ridden round most of the bumpy 37.75-mile course on a rigid-framed bike with no rear suspension in that condition — yet he was still fast enough to finish third and the stewards probably didn't have the heart to disqualify him!

In 1930 it finally all came good — though only after a last-minute addition of Birmingham's Wal Handley to the ranks of Rudge riders. Three times a TT winner, and first man to win two TT races in a single year, Handley was riding for the wealthy, but disorganised, Belgian FN team whose new Dougal Marchant-designed ohc 500 wasn't ready for the TT.

Desperate for a ride, Handley took over the entry of Rudge dealer Jim

Dr Helmut Krackowizer completed a lap of the TT course on the restored Wal Handley Rudge during the 1990 TT Parade lap. Fred Clarke peers out of the Radio TT commentry box at Ballaugh to see Dr K, at the ripe old age of 68, giving it some 'wellie' to get both wheels off the ground. (Krackowizer Collection)

ing found time to write an article describing it for 'Motor Cycling' and to register it for the road under no.JU754, put it on display as a crowd-puller in his Birmingham bike shop, managed by brother Tom.

Probably miffed because he'd won on a rival marque, FN invoked the terms of his contract to stop him racing the Rudge again, so it stayed there until 1932, when it was sold to Reg Wood of Leicester, who raced it up to the outbreak of World War Two at the local Super Speedway dirt track, both as a solo and with a sidecar fitted!

After the war, the TT-winning Rudge's descent into near-oblivion bottomed out when it was raced with a sidecar at Cadwell Park, before ending up in the hands of a VMCC member who recognised its significance — fortunately, it had remained intact and largely original all through this period. So when noted Austrian motorcycle historian, artist and Rudge guru Dr Helmut Krackowizer discovered it when he came to take part in the 1979 Millennium TT's Classic Parade, there was little missing to prevent it being brought back to Handley's race-winning trim.

Eight years later, Helmut — who used to race a Rudge himself with success in Austria and Germany after World War Two — acquired the bike on the promise that he would bring it back to British ownership after he'd commemorated Handley's TT win by riding it round the TT course one more time. After a detailed restoration to original spec by Innsbruck's Sepp Heinrich, Dr K rode the Wal Handley Rudge in the 1990 TT Parade, then offered it to the National Motorcycle Museum, which was set to buy it, but had to back out at the last minute.

Instead, the Handley Rudge has now returned to Britain as part of Brian Angliss's superb collection of historic British race bikes — but before doing so, I had the chance to ride it at Austria's glorious Osterreichring track at Zeltweg, in one of the memorable Old-TimerGP meetings organised by Helmut over the past few years.

Rudge innovation

Rudge's selection of works machinery for the 1930 TT races embodied two very different approaches. On the one hand, the 350s that dominated the Junior TT on their racing debut were a brand new, unproven hemi-head design — the famous Radial Rudge — that scored a 1-2-3 finish first time out.

By contrast, the 500cc machines that finished 1-2 in the Senior race in Rudge's most glorious IoM TT week were little different from the established GP winners of 1928/29, complete with an updated version of Pugh's proven 499cc ohv four-valve dry-sump engine design, with pent-roof combus-

Compared to the period Ulster road bike, the Handley 500 racer used a 1.5in spacer to lengthen the inlet tract on the Amal carb.

Whalley — but now he had to find a Rudge to race. With two spare machines for the three-rider team, Rudge had the equipment, but John Pugh originally declined to entrust one to Handley, on the grounds it would be unfair to his three regular team riders — Walker, Tyrell Smith and Ernie Nott, who earlier that week gave Rudge an upset 1-2-3 victory in the Junior TT with the brand-new radial four-valve racers.

However, the riders sportingly banded together to persuade Pugh to change his mind and, what's more, to give Handley the fastest bike of the five in an effort to stop Charlie Dodson and Sunbeam winning a hat trick of Senior TTs.

In a fairy tale outcome, Handley led from start to finish, to record what was to be Rudge's only Senior TT victory, and the last-ever win by a pushrod-engined motorcycle. What's more, he broke the outright lap record from a standing start on the four-valve Rudge, becoming the first man to lap the 37.75 mile Mountain Course in under half an hour, and at over 75mph.

He went on to break his own lap record twice more, before torrential rain began falling on the fourth of the seven laps. In spite of the downpour, Handley came home the winner by over three minutes from team-mate Graham Walker, at a race average speed that was actually faster than Dodson's previous lap record in the dry from the year before.

After the race, Handley acquired his TT-winning bike from Rudge and, hav-

tion chamber and twin parallel valves — each with a pair of springs and operated by rockers mounted on bolted-on support plates. Externally, this closely resembles the period Ulster road model, with the most obvious differences being the use of a one and a half inch spacer to lengthen the induction tract on the 1-5/32in Amal 10TT9 carb fitted with twin external floats. And there was a redesigned five-stud, cast-iron cylinder head with extra finning, especially in the hot-spot between the splayed exhaust ports.

The round-base, six-stud cast-iron barrel bolts via twin compression plates below the cylinder to the alloy crankcases, whose drive side casting is heavily webbed to give extra support for the flywheel assembly.

The roller-bearing crankpin supports a conrod that was a little longer for 1930 compared to the previous year's engine and, together with a forged alloy two-ring slipper piston and the plates under the cylinder, delivers 7:1 compression — ironically, a bit lower on Handley's bike than the other works Rudges that year, which ran a 7.25:1 ratio. As a result these were a little slower on top speed, though accelerated slightly better out of slower bends.

The dry sump lubrication system sees a duplex oil pump worm-driven off the timing gear, with twin filler caps on the oil tank mounted on the rear downtube. This was so that replenishment could be accomplished equally quickly either in the TT — where pit attendants had to operate on the left side of the bike — or in Continental GP races where, without exception, they worked on the right! Same rationale for the twin filler caps on the four-gallon steel fuel tank!

The 85 x 88mm engine delivers 35bhp at 5,800rpm, sparked via a single, centrally-located plug by the ML magneto mounted in front of the cylinder and gear-driven off the crank (the cut-out in the left of the fuel tank is to allow access to change the plug). This gives what is nowadays considered one of the main advantages of four-valve technology, namely a shorter flame path for improved combustion, matched by the higher revs for a given valve area delivered by the reduced reciprocating weight of lighter, paired valves, in turn yielding more power.

But back in the 1920s this was secondary to the main reason John Pugh and George Hack were originally four-valve fanatics; the improved reliability thus obtained with the relatively primitive materials of the day, due to reduced head distortion through overheating, often led to the head actually cracking. Two smaller exhaust valves run cooler than one larger one, and as well as being lighter can also be made stronger, all contributing to vital reliability.

Only later did the ancillary performance benefits become appreciated. Rudge's GP success with four-valve technology foreshadowed Honda's supremacy over 30 years later.

What's more, Pugh was an early advocate of the flatter valve angles, later requisite on performance four-stroke engine designs. The included valve angle on the Rudge pent-roof motor is about 60 degrees, at a time when most other manufacturers favoured 90 degrees or more.

Rudge's innovation didn't stop there. One of the first to fit a four-speed gearbox, they were also quickest to follow Velocette's lead in 1928 and convert the gearchange to a foot-operated positive-stop system, replacing the hand-change used hitherto. Look at the right side of the Handley bike's fuel tank, and you can see the flange which formerly supported the gate for the hand lever.

The separate gearbox has special IoM internal ratios and magnesium side - and end - covers, contributing to a dry weight with oil of 285lbs for the complete bike, in spite of the cast-iron head and barrel.

Unlike some of its contemporaries, though, Rudge paid close attention to stopping this weight properly without upsetting the handling. How? Well, firstly, the 8in drums fitted front and rear were large for the era, and with 1.5in wide shoes, have a good contact area. Secondly, to prevent such a relatively efficient front brake making the bike pull to one side when applied hard — due to its then commonplace offset position in the wheel — Rudge was the first to lace the spokes in such a way that the backplate of the brake is in the centre line of the wheel rims. Finally, pre-empting today's Honda CBR1100XX Blackbird and any Moto Guzzi V-twin by three-quarters of a century, the Rudge has linked brakes, the balance of which could be adjusted to suit each rider's individual taste.

The inverted lever at the end of the right handlebar operates the front brake alone, but the foot-pedal works both brakes via cables which can be adjusted to vary the balance. This was originally a right-foot affair for the other Rudge riders, but Handley didn't care for this so he had a Manx blacksmith make up a new one-off pedal for him before the race, which is still fitted.

Finally, Rudge made its own frames and the D-section girder forks, fitted with adjustable friction dampers in the top links and a cable-operated Bowden steering damper. The central spring box in fact contains two contra-acting individual springs, not the single shock it appears to represent.

It's not only their four-valve configuration that deserves approval. Rudges were truly avant-garde motorcycles in so many detailed ways. But road bike

Front brake worked! And Cathcart praised the couple braking system which allows the rider to stand on the rear brake for maximum stopping power or use the front lever for a touch setting up for a turn.

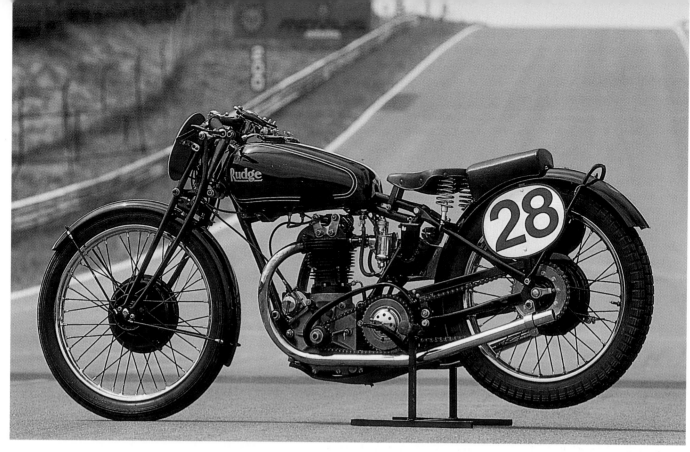

production simply wasn't big enough to underwrite the company's continued race efforts nor, ultimately, its survival after World War Two. Construction of Pugh and Hack's far-sighted projects, like an oversquare short-stroke 350 racer, or a supercharged 250 V-twin, became stillborn. But, in its day, Wal Handley's Rudge 500 was the fastest TT machine ever built.

Rideable Rudge

Before riding the Rudge I needed a lesson from Helmut Krackowizer about what all the controls do. Starting from the right, the inverted lever at the end of the handlebar operates the front brake alone (only the foot-brake on the left works the patented Rudge-Whitworth Proportionally Coupled linked brakes). Then comes the mixture control for the carb, then comes the cable adjustment for the central Bowden steering damper, on the left of which is the ignition advance/retard control. Just to the left of that is the decompressor lever for starting, while the left end inverted lever is the clutch. Lots to keep your hands busy — even after Rudge switched to a positive stop foot gearchangein 1929, and saved its riders having to grapple with a hand-change as well as the other hand controls.

Handley's TT-winning Rudge — a redesigned five-stud, cast-iron cylinder head with extra finning, especially in the hot-spot between the splayed exhaust ports .

Amazingly, you had to start the TT back then with a cold motor — you weren't allowed to start the engine and warm the oil after collecting your machine from the enclosure, so you had

to be sure it'd fire up first time at the push start, and that a full-bore cold start wouldn't damage the piston — hence the Rudge's oil feed to the back of the cylinder, to prevent the thrust face of the piston being scuffed. We did cheat a little at the O-Ring and warm the contents of the six-pint Castrol R tank — but then a practice start showed the Rudge is a ready starter, even when the decompressor wasn't working, after the cable broke when we fired it up in the paddock!

Once lit up, it pulls like a tractor from low down — there's no rev-counter, but I guess the Rudge pulls cleanly from about 1,200 rpm upwards, remarkable for a 100mph-plus 500 racer. Bottom gear of the four is strictly for starting and second is too low to have been much use anywhere except Ramsey Hairpin and Governor's Bridge, even in those days of loose surfaces and a narrower, tighter TT Course.

However, there's a big gap to third, with fourth very close to that — a fact later confirmed by a copy of Handley's magazine article, quoting 4.4, 4.8, 6.3 and 8.75 as the gearbox ratios in the bike chosen by the works team for the IoM. That turned out to be just as well, because worn dogs (or perhaps an inherent fault of the primitive positive stop change mechanism) meant fourth gear popped out occasionally — not badly, because it engages again almost at once, but enough to discover that the Rudge will lap the O-Ring almost as fast in third gear as it will using fourth everywhere except the Hella-S chicane and Bosch Kurve. It's very high geared. Cutting down on changing gear was a good thing as far as I was concerned, though — not because the action is stiff or vague (it isn't), but because I detested the heel and toe change lever later copied by a generation of 1950s Italian lightweights. Operating this means you have to lift your foot off the rest high enough to heel down through the gears, making it desirable to do all your changing gear in a straight line, while not having to worry about using body pressure to change direction or control the bike over bumps.

As a works racer straddling the two eras, the Rudge has a gearshift only slightly less convenient than a hand-lever, but a power unit that is as flexi-ble and friendly as it could be. It's rela-tively high-revving for a long-stroke single of that era, and feels to have sur-prisingly little inertia, so it picks up revs easily. It's also extremely smooth, a fact which is as much a credit to restorer Sepp Heinrich's handiwork as to John Pugh's design — whatever the balance factor is, it's dead right. However, there's lots of torque, and great acceleration out of the Zeltweg chicane, so maybe the Rudge doesn't have quite the same top-end power as a cammy racer of the Vintage era. It certainly felt as if it was struggling a lit-tle topped out, though that might equally as well have been down to carb jetting not being right for the Styrian hills of Austria.

However, the Rudge's trump card was still to be played. Much to my surprise the handling of the rigid-framed, girder-forked bike is really excellent — even over the several patches of ripples and bumps left by fat-tired touring cars on the Zeltweg track. It steers beautifully — light and easy, but quite predictable — with the Rudge D-forks doing a good job even by post-war standards soaking up quite pronounced road shock. Back at base after my first session on the bike, I relayed this opinion to Helmut, who beamed in agreement. "In my opinion, this is the best design of girder fork," he enthuses. "It's only equalled, not surpassed, by the Webb forks on a Velocette KTT. The Rudge steers like a bicycle, whereas in comparison, a Garden Gate Norton handles like an elephant! The top and bottom links on the Rudge are one-piece, so very stiff, and the sprung damper works very well."

But the relatively smooth '90s Tarmac race track is a very different proposition from the Mountain Course of 1930. Still, in the course of an invigorating dice with a later Rudge Ulster and a KTT Velo, I certainly rode the Handley Rudge hard enough to be impressed by

how expertly it rode over bumps when pressed. I also came away full of praise for the brakes, by far the best I've ever sampled on a Vintage era racer. Quite simply, they work! The Rudge stops really well, and I have to say I quite liked the coupled brakes on this bike, even if I don't care for them on modern ones with more effective stoppers. On the Rudge, the system gives you the benefit of being able to get maximum stopping power just by standing on the foot pedal, whereas if you just want a touch on the brakes to set yourself up for a turn, you just use the front lever. The coupled system works so well that you must take care not to get the back end stepping out by being too heavy-footed on the angle — not a criticism I've ever had of Vintage brakes on a Tarmac course!

Words: *Alan Cathcart,*
Photos: *Kyoichi Nakamura*

Handlebar control layout is... busy. And that's after Rudge had switched to a positive stop foot gearchange in 1929!

Dr Helmut Krackowizer with the machine he painstakingly restored to its original glory.

Jimmy Simpson

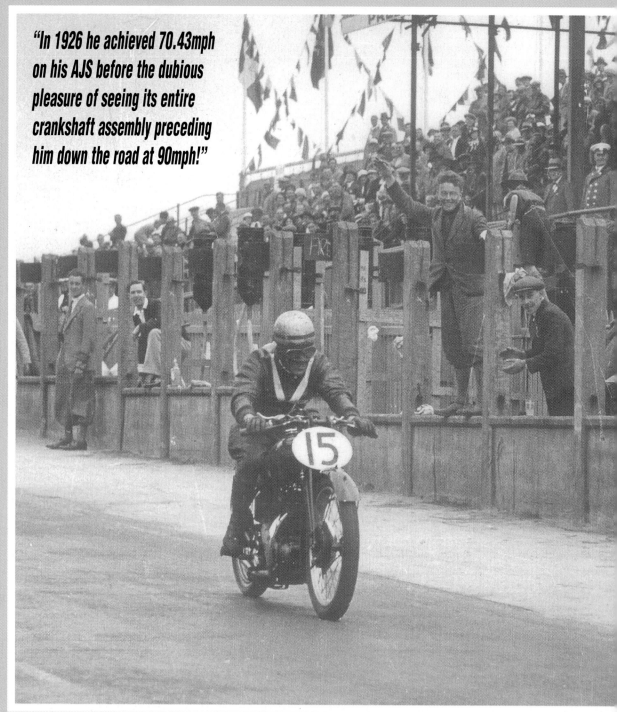

"In 1926 he achieved 70.43mph on his AJS before the dubious pleasure of seeing its entire crankshaft assembly preceding him down the road at 90mph!"

Jimmy Simpson crosses the line to record his solitary TT win — the 1934 Lightweight on a 250cc Rudge. (Mick Woollett Archive)

J H Simpson — universally known to his thousands of future admirers as 'Jimmy' — was born in Handsworth, Birmingham, in June 1898. His family on both sides were in comfortable middle-class circumstances. Jimmy's childhood was uneventful, and on the whole, a happy one. An early interest in motorcycles was stimulated when his maternal grandfather became an agent for the new Rudge in about 1910. As soon as Jimmy was old enough to hold a licence (14 in those days) he was given a 500cc

Rudge with which he soon earned a reputation, riding in the speed trials and speed hill climbs of the day. (For that matter, so did his mother, but she did not go on to become a world famous TT rider!)

The 1914 war saw both Jimmy and his father (to whom he was close) volunteering quite independently to serve their country.

Demobilised in 1919, Jimmy was taken on by AJS Motorcycles of Wolverhampton as a tester. AJS was then working on the famous 350cc ohv

TT models that were to revolutionise motorcycle racing in the next few years, and it was Jimmy's fervent hope to become a works rider.

However, the company had the pick of a dozen well-established and experienced men and there was no room for Jimmy in the team. Disgusted, he left, and took a job — nothing to do with motorcycles — on the Gold Coast of Africa! Returning to England after a year or so, he went to work for AJS agent Wilf Chapman in Leicester, and quickly re-established a reputation in

Pacesetter

Jimmy Simpson was fast. He was the first man to hit a 60mph lap around the TT course. He was the first to 70 — and 80. But a TT victory eluded him until 1934.

but throughout his career was a first-class trials rider up to and including Gold in the ISDT. He raced at Brooklands and was also famous for racing on sand — a popular sport in the 1920s. He also proved to be an excellent development engineer whom the racing department soon began to value, first at AJS, and later under Joe Craig at Norton.

Jimmy's racing career spanned 13 years from 1922 to 1934. During that time he was entered in 26 TT races on the Isle of Man (including an uncharacteristic sidecar entry with George Rowley in the chair in 1925. The machine was a 350cc AJS and despite giving away 250cc to the other contenders, they came home in fifth place).

Of his 25 solo TT rides, he finished only nine times — four times for AJS, four times for Norton and once for Rudge. He had his share of accidents and mishaps on the Island, but more often than not, especially with AJS, mechanical failure was his reason for retirement. During his career he set no fewer than eight fastest laps and was the first to achieve speeds of over 60mph, 70mph and 80mph! These were in 1924 when he hoisted his own Junior lap record by all but 5mph to 64.54mph in a year when Freddy Dixon's fastest Senior lap on the Douglas was 63.75mph!

In 1926 he achieved 70.43mph on his Senior AJS before having the dubious pleasure of seeing its entire crankshaft assembly preceding him down the road

the sprints and speed hill climbs (held in those days on closed public roads), so popular in the early 1920s. So well did he perform that Wilf Chapman had no difficulty in persuading AJS to promise a TT ride for Jimmy in the 1922 Junior race.

For whatever reason, Jimmy turned down the offer! Instead, he urged Chapman to have rival Leicester dealer and Scott agent Harold Petty provide a 500cc two-stroke twin for the Senior race. Petty went one better, and it was on a genuine factory Scott that Jimmy

made his TT debut. Alas, it was no fairy tale — though he passed five earlier starters on the road, the Scott split its petrol tank wide open and Jimmy was out of the race by Kirkmichael on the first lap!

However, brief as his race had been, he had impressed a lot of people, including the directors of AJS. He was offered his old job as a tester and a works ride, and now that the 'boot was on the other foot' he accepted.

Jimmy, let it be understood, was not only a wonderfully skilful road racer,

Jimmy Simpson Pacesetter

Simpson at Quarter Bridge on a 350cc Norton during the 1934 Junior TT. He finished second to team-mate Jimmy Guthrie — beaten by just nine seconds. (Mick Woollett Archive)

at about 90mph!

His 80+mph record lap was with his Senior Norton in 1931 and was in fact 80.82mph. Other fastest laps came in the 1923 Junior at 59.59mph, the 1925 Senior at 68.97mph and the Junior at 67.94mph — all on AJS machinery. On his Senior Norton in 1932 he recorded 81.50mph, and on a 250cc Rudge in the 1934 Lightweight TT (which he won) 73.64mph.

His actual TT placings for AJS were all in the Junior class, in 1925 third, second in 1926 and third again 1927. In the Senior class for Norton he was third in 1930 and again in 1932. He was second in the Senior in 1933 and 1934 and second in the 1934 Junior.

Between 1924 and 1927, he scored no less than eight wins in the Grand Prix — the 350cc classes of the Italian Grand Prix at Monza in 1924, in the French Grand Prix in 1925, in the 500cc class in Belgium in 1926, and thereafter in the 350cc class in Germany. In his best year with AJS, 1927, he won the 350cc classes (and made fastest laps) in Germany, Belgium, Switzerland and Austria.

He also won no less than 11 Grand Prix events for Norton in the five years between 1930 and 1934. After his successes of 1927 things turned sour at AJS.

He walked away from AJS (where one senses that relationships had been edgy on both sides) straight into welcoming arms at Norton, in Bracebridge Street. There, he was to provide valu-

able inputs into the brand new Joe Craig/Arthur Carroll engine that was to dominate racing in the 1930s.

Alas, his first outing at the 1929 TT was disastrous when he was involved in the notorious pile-up at Greeba in which Norton rider Doug Lamb lost his life and which ended Jack Ammott's road racing career for Rudge. His injuries were enough to keep Jimmy out of racing for the rest of 1929. The new Norton engine proved willing, powerful and reliable, but at 450lbs the machine was grossly handicapped.

With Joe Craig's approval, Jimmy managed to cut that weight by an astonishing 130lbs and was rewarded by a win in the 500cc class of the 1930 Swedish Grand Prix. In 1932, he won the 350cc classes in France and Belgium, in 1933 in France and Sweden. In 1934 things finally came good for Jimmy. Not only did he finish second in the Junior and Senior TTs, but he also achieved his life-long ambition, to win a TT. This he did

on a 250cc Rudge provided (the factory being in receivership at the time) by Graham Walker's 'Racing Syndicate'.

After a monumental blow-up in practise, Jimmy did not start in the happiest frame of mind, his gloom being exacerbated by the dreadfully wet and misty conditions. His goggles became wet on the inside and at the end of the first lap he pulled into his pit to retire.

Norton's Dennis Mansell wouldn't hear of it. Producing a fresh pair of goggles, he sent Jimmy on his way and to eventual rejoicing. Even so, it seems a pity that Jimmy never won a Senior TT. However, he won the 350cc races in Holland, Germany, Switzerland and Belgium. He also won the 500cc race in Belgium — the only 'double' of his career. And for his swan song, he won the 350cc race of the Ulster Grand Prix in which success had always eluded him. Remarkably, he made fastest lap in every one of those six Grand Prix. What was there left to prove? At 36 years of age, Jimmy Simpson probably had a few further successful years' riding in his grasp but he was nothing if not realistic. He was happy to join Shell Mex as Competition Manager, a post he fulfilled with great credit.

The outbreak of World War Two in 1939 saw Jimmy in the Army again, this time with a Commission.

Post-war, he rejoined Shell Mex, and was to be seen at all the major motorcycling events, a genial and congenial figure immaculately dressed in grey flannels, navy blue blazer with a silk foulard around his neck.

He finally retired to Cornwall, in the mid-1960s, hale and hearty. He died in his 84th year, shortly after sharing a couple of bottles of champagne with a friend. Few figures in motorcycle racing were more respected, admired and welcomed company than the legendary Jimmy Simpson.

Words: Brian Woolley

Three TT 'greats': Jimmy Simpson (left) with Ernie Nott (centre) and Graham Walker after the 1934 Lightweight TT in which they finished 1-2-3 respectively on Rudges. (Mick Woollett Archive)